REN ZHENGFEI

&

HUAWEI

A BUSINESS AND LIFE BIOGRAPHY

Published by
LID Publishing Limited
One Adam Street, London WC2N 6LE

31 West 34th Street, 8th Floor, Suite 8004,
New York, NY 10001, US

info@lidpublishing.com
www.lidpublishing.com

A member of:

BPR
Business Publishers Roundtable

www.businesspublishersroundtable.com

Published in collaboration with the China Translation & Publishing House (a member of the China Publishing Group Corporation)

CTPH China Translation and Publishing House

© LID Publishing Limited, 2017
© China Translation and Publishing House, 2017

Printed in Great Britain by TJ International
ISBN: 978-1-911498-29-2

Illustration: Myriam El Jerari
Cover and page design: Caroline Li

REN ZHENGFEI
&
HUAWEI

A BUSINESS AND LIFE BIOGRAPHY

BY **LI HONGWEN**

LONDON   MONTERREY
MADRID   SHANGHAI
MEXICO CITY   BOGOTA
NEW YORK   BUENOS AIRES
BARCELONA   SAN FRANCISCO

CONTENTS

PRELUDE

A statistical study carried out by the Tsinghua National Entrepreneurship Research Center shows that the best age for startup entrepreneurs is between 26 and 35 years old, and 40 years old marks the end of entrepreneurship.

In 1987, the 43 year-old Ren Zhengfei retired from a People's Liberation Army (PLA) base in Sichuan, and came to work for the Shenzhen Nanyou Group as the deputy manager in its affiliated electronics company.

Honesty helped Ren Zhengfei navigate through eleven military years. However, sabotage quickly taught him the guileful nature of the business realm. Duped into a bad deal, the company found itself in debt of over two million yuan. In this situation, Ren Zhengfei had no choice but to bite the bullet and leave Nanyou, truly unemployed.

When it rains, it pours and his first wife left him soon after. At that time, Ren Zhengfei was under a great strain to take care of his retired parents and help his six younger brothers and sisters.

With the resilience of a soldier and eleven years' military education, Ren Zhengfei did not crumble in the face of these challenges. With no time to brood over the business failure or family break up, Ren Zhengfei decisively started a business in 1988. He started a small technology company, Huawei, with only 20 thousand yuan, getting off to a rocky start by selling a Hong Kong (HK) made telecom switchboard. After fifteen years' of hard work, Huawei's sales revenue reached 30 billion USD in 2003. Huawei was a dominant force amongst the most successful national companies of China.

Ren Zhengfei did not forget that when he first started Huawei, his parents, his siblings and himself were living in a crowded 12-square-metres house where the balcony was used as a makeshift kitchen. His parents would go to the market before closing time to buy cheap vegetables and fish or shrimp to scrape together enough food to survive.

Difficulty leads to greatness. But after having achieved great success, Zhengfei did not forget his indigent youth: the six brothers and sisters depending entirely on their parents' meagre wages. Starvation was the norm, and to have a white flour bread bun was the greatest luxury he had longed for.

Ren Zhengfei didn't forget the 150 thousand employees standing behind him, shining with ideals and entrepreneurial spirit. He established a "joint stock for all" initiative to extend the development dividend to everyone.

Whether in the midst of financial turmoil, the IT bubble, and pressure from international industry giants or brutal domestic competition, Ren Zhengfei remained strong. Clenching the steering wheel of an aircraft carrier of private telecoms, Huawei, to cut through rapids and torrents, and forge ahead.

In 2007, with an annual revenue of 125.6 billion USD, Huawei became the fifth largest telecom company worldwide.

In 2010, Huawei debuted on the Fortune Global 500 list, ranking 29th in IT corporations, out of the 397 companies listed in total.

In 2011, Ren Zhengfei entered Forbes World's Billionaires List for the first time with a net worth of 1.1 billion USD, ranking 1,056 globally, and 92nd in China.

In 2012, Fortune magazine listed Ren Zhengfei among the top of the most influential business leaders in China, a category he then secured first place in only one year later.

In 2013, Huawei achieved an annual sales revenue of 2,390,250 billion RMB, an increase of 85%. Huawei's smart phone business made a historic breakthrough into the global top three brands, and its global brand awareness increased by 110%. In the spring breeze of the reform and opening up era, Huawei's employees understood taking stock and seizing the opportunity, to expand and strengthen the enterprise with the strategy of using rural areas to encircle the city. They were as alert as Bei,[1] swinging into action like a wolf. When a business opportunity arose, they would act immediately, with eyes on the target, to win.

Today, Huawei's products and solutions are very comprehensive, covering mobile, core network, value-added telecom services, terminals and other fields.

In India, USA, Sweden, Russia and many cities in China including Beijing, Shanghai and Nanjing, Huawei set up a number of research institutes. By the end of 2013, Huawei had more than 36,500 patents, setting the record for the largest number of patent applications among China's domestic enterprises for years.

Despite his overwhelming prestige, Ren Zhengfei keeps a low profile, and even excused himself from the position of vice chairman of the All-China Federation of Industry and Commerce and as the deputy to the National People's Congress, which are vied for by entrepreneurs. A Chinese reporter once bemoaned, "It is far more difficult to get an interview with him than Li Ka-shing, the richest Chinese person in the world."

No matter how reclusive Ren Zhengfei remains, he continues to be in the media spotlight. The interest about Ren Zhengfei and Huawei is ceaseless: according to some, he is mysterious, while others see him as a 'coyote', or simple and crude, or empathizing and righteous. To some he is a soldier and to others his heroic spirit is complemented by his tender heart. Whether receiving praise or slander, Ren Zhengfei ignores what is said and chooses not to respond, because for him no response is the best response.

Onlookers have the most to say: *Time* magazine has described Huawei as a company that is repeating the steps of Cisco, Ericsson and other globally influential companies, and is becoming the most dangerous rival of these telecom giants; *The Economist* has asserted that the rise of Huawei means catastrophe for foreign multinational corporations.

The Italian media has added fuel to these claims and, according *la Repubblica* magazine, the global sales of Huawei exceeded 35.4 billion USD in 2012, with an increase of 8% year-on-year, of which 66% was from overseas markets. Huawei may surpass its competitor, Ericsson, to become the world's largest telecom equipment supplier ...

It is a beautiful picture to look forward to!

---

1. Bei is a wolf-like animal in old Chinese folktales.

CHAPTER

1

HARD YOUTH

Money can't buy hard youth.
– Zhu Guangqian

Childhood hardships and tribulations can become a valuable asset in one's life. Starvation and poverty push the tree of life to root down to the earth. The deeper the root spans, the bigger the tree will grow to be.

THE POOR AND GRAY-COLOURED CHILDHOOD

Longing for vacation, for tomorrow,
for outgrowing childhood.
– Childhood by Luo Dayou

Ren Zhengfei's ancestral home is in Rendian village, Huang-chai, a major town in the Pujiang county, Jinhua, Zhejiang. Rendian village had a small number of tenants by the end of the Qing dynasty (1644 to 1912) and the start of republics; men and women fulfilled their roles in ploughing farms or weaving. Country folks were simple and honest in the peaceful neighbourhoods.

In front of the village flows the clear and graceful Pu River. Guanyan Mountain crouches in the background like an awe-inspiring lion. There is beautiful scenery, with trees, flowers and bamboo inside the village.

The Rens were a large and prominent family in Ren-dian village. Ren Sanhe, the grandfather of Ren Zhengfei, was a master of curing Jinhua ham. When he moiled in old Pujiang county, the ham he made had crystal yellow skin, ruddy flesh and a rich aroma. His unique technique carried his name far and wide. Therefore, Ren Sanhe's family was affluent in Rendian village. Their old house was in a high-ranking courtyard. To carve the window patterns alone took the carpenter three full years.

Ren Sanhe got married and had a son, Moxun. Ren Moxun was bright, and remembered everything he read or wrote. Happiness surged in Ren Sanhe's heart. In order to nurture his son's potential, Ren Sanhe sent him to university in Peking.

Ren Moxun became the first university student in Rendian village. This was as glorious as achieving the status of Juren, which was a civil service examination system in Imperial China to select candidates for the state bureaucracy.

Ren Moxun studied in the Economics Department in Peking Minzu University. Meanwhile, he joined the Communist Youth League, and took to the streets with ardent youth, campaigning for anti-Japanese and Save the Nation movements. However, this was impermanent. Ren Moxun's parents died in quick succession, and he lost his means of paying for university. Ren Moxun dropped out of university and returned home. He became a teacher and taught in the Dinghai Fishery Vocational School and Nanjing Agricultural Vocational School to earn a living.

In December 1937, the Japanese took Nanjing by storm. The Chinese nation was at a critical point. With a chest of hot blood, Ren Moxun went to work at the Kuomintang (KMT, the Nationalist Party of China) 412 military factory as an accountant. It was a specialized military factory for producing gas masks. Ren Moxun worked for the KMT military, but he identified and supported the Communist Party's Unite the Nation and resist Japanese invaders.

He not only promoted anti-Japanese ideals but also organized a book club to discuss issues regarding the Anti-Japanese War. This caused issues as his patriotic actions peaked the attention of Kuomintang special agents.

Due to changes in the war situation, the military factory was moved to Tongzi, Guizhou through Guangxi. In 1944, Ren Moxun detected the threatening changes and left the military factory with the excuse of sending family back to his hometown. However, Kuomintang special agents shadowed him like phantoms. Remarkably, they took the wrong person. The next day, Ren Moxun feigned sickness and asked the villagers to carry him in a pilong (similar to a sedan chair) to the Zhengjiawu railway station, freeing himself from the clutches of the Kuomintang special agents. He then left his hometown for Guizhou, a province in southwest China.

To avoid persecution by the Kuomintang agents, Ren Moxun stayed in Zhenning County, a mountainous region in Anshun, Guizhou. The typical karst terrain led to the creation of the famous Huangguoshu Waterfall. However, tourism was a foreign word at that time and life in the Zhenning mountains was very difficult.

Here Ren Moxun met seventeen-year-old Cheng Yuanzhao. They fell in love and got married. Shortly afterwards, on 25 October 1944, a healthy boy was born into the family and brought them immense joy.

While holding the loud crying baby boy, Ren Moxun said to Cheng Yuanzhao, who was confined to bed after birth: "I want to give our son a meaningful name."

Cheng Yuanzhao asked: "What shall we name him?"

Ren Moxun thought for a while: "We'll name him Ren Zhengfei."

"That's a good name." Cheng Yuanzhao took her son from her husband's arms, and said affectionately: "You have a name. You are Ren Zhengfei."

Cheng Yuanzhao grew up in the mountains and was cheerful and sincere. In the poverty-stricken mountainous areas of Guizhou, Cheng Yuanzhao's parents supported her to graduate from high school. With some assistance from her husband, she educated herself and became a maths teacher.

The couple had a total of two sons and five daughters, of which Ren Zhengfei was the oldest. The family of nine lived on their modest teaching salaries, and Ren Moxun would also send money back to his hometown every month for his family.

During the war-torn times, life was destitute. The parents in the Ren house could give their children bright minds, but could not afford enough food or warm clothes. In order to make sure their seven children had books to read, Ren Zhengfei's parents would be careful with their money and sometimes have to borrow some. Despite this, they did not feel bitter about life.

SCHOOL TIME: HERCULES INSPIRATION

A peasant in the farmhouse in the morning, reached imperial court by evening; Generals or Ministers are not born in their standing, this is something which men should aspire to.
–Verse of Prodigy

The first elementary school Ren Zhengfei enrolled in was a mountain village school close to his home. The ramshackle classrooms foretold the bitter conditions awaiting the children. Summer was steaming and stuffy, bugs and mosquitoes hummed all around. Though wood burned in the iron stove in winter, the wind would penetrate the classroom, levelling the inside temperature to roughly that of the outside.

Ren Zhengfei was carefree as a youth; playing was his nature. Though, he gradually gave in to studying hard. For inspiration, Cheng Yuanzhao read the story of Hercules to her son.

Zeus, the king of gods, had a son named Hercules with the beautiful Alcmene. In vengeance, Zeus' wife Hera tried to kill Hercules.

While no one was around, Hera stealthily put two snakes into the cradle of the little Hercules. Hercules woke up from a dream seeing the poisonous snakes approaching him with bared fangs. He stretched out his two small hands and suddenly caught the two snakes, one in each hand. When Zeus arrived, the snakes had been killed by Hercules.

Little Hercules grew up robustly in the shadow of Hera's murderous threat. He grew to be tall and strong, noble and dignified. He became a well-known hero and built the name Hercules into one of prestige.

After Hercules grew up, his mother decided to let him leave home to trek to far off places. To escape the cruel retaliation from Hera was one reason; the second was to fortify him against a variety of difficult hardships. Before his leaving, Hercules' mother asked him to complete 12 tasks that others could not imagine in order to temper his will and fortify his skills.

Cheng Yuanzhao stopped here deliberately. Ren Zhengfei pried anxiously: "Did Hercules complete the 12 tasks?"

Cheng Yuanzhao looked at her anxious son and said: "The following part is very exciting. If you want to hear it, you need to get good test scores, and then I will continue to tell the story." Though young and playful, Ren Zhengfei knew what his mother meant. Ren Zhengfei achieved excellent grades in primary school by modelling himself on his own well-educated father, being enlightened by his diligent and virtuous mother, and by applying his own effort.

When Ren Zhengfei brought home a satisfactory school report card, Cheng Yuanzhao praised her son and told him the end of Hercules' story.

The 12 unimaginable tasks were eventually completed, and Hercules held the grand Olympic Games in Olympia to celebrate the victory. His fame resounded in every corner of the world.

Though still young, Ren Zhengfei understood the lesson his mother wanted him to learn from the end of this story: Hercules made his name by doing good deeds for humanity. Ren Zhengfei quietly made the following resolution: to study hard and grow into Hercules, to do great things for mankind, to pursue the value and glory of life.

GOING TO UNIVERSITY: THE TURNING POINT OF LIFE

People admire the dazzling splendour of success, but forget its bud is soaked in the tears of struggle and sprinkled by the blood of sacrifice.
– Bing Xin

Ren Zhengfei's schooling was riddled with struggles, wanting for food and clothes.

The geography of the land in Guizhou makes it unsuitable for farming. Many places in the region are deficient of food production. However, during the years of the Great Leap Forward campaign of the Communist Party of China (CPC) – a campaign set to transform the country through industrialization and collectivization – people blindly gave false production numbers. This resulted in inadequate food production, because high recruitment was specified for the region from the central government based on these false production numbers. In 1960, there were serious signs of famine in Guizhou. Some local leaders, however, for personal reasons, still reported to higher officials the 'progressive experiences' of the public canteen across the whole province. A lie repeated a thousand times becomes the truth, but this lie crumbled to pieces in the face of hunger. The public canteen in rural Guizhou came to an end in 1961.

At that time, Ren Zhengfei was 18 years old and studied in the county high school. His desperate desire for learning and knowledge threw him into countless books, as he was interested in feeding his mind, not just his stomach. The greatest luxury he longed for in high school was a delicious white flour bread bun.

Even though they experienced various hardships, Ren Zhengfei's parents insisted on sending their seven children to school to become useful people in society. Conscious of having to save money for Ren Zhengfei's college prospects, his mother, after careful deliberation, decided to strictly serve individualized dining. No one was full, but it ensured that everyone stayed alive.

In the battle against hunger, Ren Zhengfei's mother would lead the children to pick up red thorn fruits from the mountain. They would also tame a rocky patch of the mountain and plant pumpkins to survive the famine. They also accidentally discovered that the fleshy canna roots near their land could be cooked to fill their stomachs.

Every night, the boys and girls of the Ren family sat around the stove, waiting for a pot of canna roots or pumpkins cooked by their mother. There was little nutrition, and they would still be hungry after a while, but they could taste sweetness in the insubstantial food as they ate in the glow of their loving family.

Ren Zhengfei set his mind on studying and got good grades. The school always praised his aptitude. In high school, he was growing so fast, but due to hunger, he experienced lethargy. Dizzy spells affected his academic performance, which had its ups and downs and was as unpredictable as a roller coaster. He had to re-take a few tests to pass the second year of high school. To save energy and be able to study for the college entrance examination in his senior year, Ren Zhengfei came up with a way to make pancakes out of rice bran and vegetables. The bran pancake was bitter and rough and was difficult to swallow. One day, when Ren Zhengfei was eating the pancakes, Ren Moxun saw him and said in shock: "Zhengfei … you can't eat this. You will harm your body."

Nonchalantly, Ren Zhengfei replied: "It's nothing. I am young, and healthy."

Ren Moxun took Ren Zhengfei's hand and shook his head, his heart aching. Every morning, Cheng Yuanzhao would give Ren Zhengfei a little piece of corn bread, and would tell him to study hard for his entrance exams.

Hard work paid off. Ren Zhengfei, not overwhelmed by any difficulties, passed the college entrance examination. He was admitted to the Chongqing Institute of Architecture and Engineering, which had the impactful resources of academic staff and laboratory equipment. It was one of the eight most prestigious old architecture schools in China.

Ren Zhengfei graduated from high school and was admitted into university, which meant he was no longer a young boy, but had become a man. He could weather all kinds of storms and face different challenges all by himself.

During the times of economic difficulty, each individual had a quota for clothing coupons. Despite this, Cheng

Yuanzhao took up a needle and thread and made two new shirts for her son. Ren Zhengfei took the neatly sewn, crisp new shirts with tears surging in his eyes. He knew that for these two white shirts, his brothers and sisters would probably need to wear old clothes for a long time, and tighten their belts.

To attend the Chongqing Institute Ren Zhengfei also needed a bed sheet. This was not a problem for Cheng Yuanzhao. She picked up a few old sheets dumped by graduates, cleaned them, cut them and stitched them together to make a new bed sheet.

The two shirts and the stitched together bed sheet accompanied Ren Zhengfei for five years, until he finished his college life in Chongqing.

CHAPTER

MILITARY LIFE

Those serving in the army are upright men.
– General Barton

After Ren Zhengfei graduated from the Chongqing Institute of Architecture and Engineering, he responded to the call of the country, proudly enlisting in the Capital Construction Engineering Corporation.

Ren Zhengfei was assigned to an aircraft manufacturing plant. Here he was dedicated to research, and two of his research results filled the scientific gaps of the national industry. While his achievements were acclaimed, and he rolled up his sleeves, the Capital Construction Engineering Corporation was cancelled due to disarmament.

Ren Zhengfei made a huge transition from soldier to businessman. This transformation of roles was significant for him. After he moved on to work for the Shenzhen Nanyou Group, he encountered a low point which would impact his life immensely.

JOINING THE ARMY: AMBITIOUS TO SERVE THE COUNTRY

Rather to be a centurion, better than an intellectual.
– Yang Jiong

In 1963, the 19 year-old Ren Zhengfei lived up to his parents' expectations and went to study in Chongqing. He left his high school in the remote mountainous county and entered the hustle and bustle of Chongqing. Learning new things in this delightful atmosphere made him feel like a fish roaming blithely in the ocean of knowledge.

With only one year left before graduation, the nationwide catastrophe of the Cultural Revolution began. Rebels were engaged in taking over factories, schools and villages. Posters were plastered all over the walls in colleges. Presidents and professors, who were denounced in gatherings one after another, were overthrown. The scene was extremely intense. In this frenzied movement, only a few students could settle down into the benches in the classrooms.

Ren Zhengfei was the exception. He took his books and learned what he was supposed to, bit by bit. He even taught himself seemingly irrelevant courses like computer science, digital technology and automation. Even his family said that working hard on these irrelevant courses was respectful and touching.

Ren Zhengfei was also acquainted with a few professors from Xi'an Jiaotong University, from whom he would get books to read. In addition, he carried out strenuous advanced mathematics exercises from beginning to end, and taught himself philosophy and logic, as well as English and Japanese, to the extent that he could at least read the college textbooks for those languages. Even today, when Ren Zhengfei inspects European or American markets, he can negotiate business with local clients directly in English, without any help from a translator.

After graduation, Ren Zhengfei first worked in construction. In 1974, the nation tried to achieve industrial modernization as soon as possible. An advanced chemical fibre system was introduced, with a total investment of 2.8 billion yuan, and a counterparts factory was built in the city of Liaoyang. To ensure the successful foundation of the chemical fibre base in Liaoyang, many different types of skilled people were urgently recruited and mobilized nationwide. However, they needed to join the army first, and then participated in the project in the form of military support.

Ren Zhengfei put on the uniform and joined the army in 1974 as a member of the Capital Construction Engineering Corporation in the Liaoyang construction site. The Capital Construction Engineering Corporation is a unique arm of services in China, serving large and medium-sized national construction projects. It began on 1 August 1966 and developed to encompass 10 units of corporations and 500,000 soldiers, a true commando in the frontline of national infrastructure construction.

Due to his technical knowledge, Ren Zhengfei was selected to join the signal corporation, and transferred to an aircraft manufacturing plant in Anshun, Guizhou to participate in developing a military communications system with the code name 011. Ren Zhengfei was motivated and studied assiduously. He also completed a series of inventions, two of which filled technology gaps of the nation at that time.

While serving in the military, Ren Zhengfei got married. A married man becomes truly mature, like a sailing boat finding the harbour. When Ren Zhengfei got married, his family was still experiencing financial difficulties, but his brothers and sisters scraped together 100 yuan to help him and his wife begin their life together. It was not much, but it was testament to the deep true love among the Ren brothers and sisters.

Ren Zhengfei spent many years in the military. In addition to technological inventions, he also studied Marx's *Capital* and four volumes of the *Selected Works* of Mao Zedong. The core of these was deeply imprinted in his mind, and was later referred to in Huawei's operations and management, establishing the unique corporate management culture of Huawei.

With the arrival of 1982, Ren Zhengfei's military life came to an end. Due to the restructuring of the national economy and the reform of the military system, the Party Central Committee decided to revoke the Capital

Construction Engineering Corporation. Since Ren Zheng-fei was the technical asset of the troops, leaders wished for him to stay and prepared to transfer him to another research base. Ren Zhengfei gave this a lot of thought, and despite this option he finally made the difficult decision of leaving. For better prospects for his children, Ren Zhengfei decided he had to bid goodbye to military life.

Ren Zhengfei's wife had taken the first step to working at management level in Shenzhen Nanyou Group before him. He went through the release procedures subsequently, and took his son and daughter south, to the young and vibrant border city of Shenzhen.

Shenzhen Nanyou Group was founded in 1984, and was responsible for the construction, development and comprehensive management of 23 square kilometres of land in the south of the Shenzhen Peninsula, where the largest industrial park in Shenzhen was located. After years of expansion, Shenzhen Nanyou Group became the biggest enterprise in the municipal city, and made tremendous contributions to the Shenzhen special economic zone.

Ren Zhengfei's daughter, Meng Wanzhou, who took her mother's family name, reportedly said that life was harsh when they arrived at Shenzhen. They lived in a house where the wind would cut through walls in all directions, the rain would leak through the roof – a rainy day outside would be a rainy day inside as well.

But with his military background, Ren Zhengfei never feared harsh environments. He clenched his fists and rolled up his sleeves, eager to dive in. He was like a bow pulled taunt, ready to shoot his arrow into new goals: he wanted to aspire to his dreams and give his family a good life. He had the feeling that his goals would be achieved in this city.

FAILURE: BEARING THE BITTER ALONE

Failure is the last test of perseverance.
– Bismarck

Wheeling and dealing create a constant blur in the business world. Ren Zhengfei was respectable and honest, loyal to friends and genuine to everyone. However, his military legacy did not prepare him for vulnerabilities in business. He was defrauded by a business partner by approximately 2 million yuan debt uncollectible: this was his first encounter of the hardships of business.

He had to sell everything to pay the debt, and lost his job in the Nanyou Group forever. Ren Zhengfei was unemployed.

At the same time, his first marriage ended in tandem with this hardship. After divorce, he rented a very small house with his parents and nephew. There was no kitchen in the house, and the balcony was used for cooking. Ren Zhengfei was tired, in mind and body. He stayed up late every night, unable to stop wondering and pondering over what would happen in the future.

Ren Zhengfei wanted to start his own business, and not on a small scale. In 1987, he, along with his partners, founded Shenzhen Huawei Technologies Company with 20,000 yuan in registered capital. Later, when people asked him the meaning of 'Huawei', Ren Zhengfei replied: "'Hua' means 'China'. 'Wei' means 'to achieve'. China can achieve."

To rent an office building for Huawei would cost a few thousand a month. Apartments, on the contrary, were cheap, three to four hundred at most. Ren Zhengfei understood the difficulties involved in the start-up. He didn't rent an office building or decorate a splendid office for himself. He started his business in crude settings.

Huawei was registered as a collective enterprise. Though having technology in its name, it started with trade business. Through the introduction of friends, it started to sell industrial devices needed by factories and mines, like fire alarm devices and gas bearing gyroscopes. However, the number of orders was too small to sustain the daily operations of the company. Ren Zhengfei put all his hope in the small HAX switchboard made by the Hong Kong Hongnian Company, though he knew that he didn't have the capital to make a deposit on the investment.

So, Ren Zhengfei decided to contact the owner of Hongnian – like attracted like – and the owner was very impressed by Ren Zhengfei's personality and genuine talk. The owner of Hongnian generously authorized credit for Ren Zhengfei, which allowed him to get small HAX switchboards while paying in advance.

Huawei made big profits on small HAX switchboards because of the price margin. Even after Huawei transformed into a business giant, with annual sales of 30 billion USD, Ren Zhengfei did not forget the kindness of the owner of Hongnian, who had helped him in his desperate time. During the Hong Kong economic recession, Ren Zhengfei helped him pull through various crises.

In the 1980s, the penetration of telephones in the Chinese market was low. In a country with over a billion people, only one person among hundreds had a telephone, and the installation fee for each was 5,000 yuan. Money could not get you a telephone immediately, you needed to enter the queuing system, and the waiting time could be from three months to a year. Some people even invited officials and higher-ups to dinners and sent them gifts in order to get their telephone installed earlier. The problem was that there were not enough connection ports in switchboards to support more telephones working.

The effectiveness of the HAX switchboard was superior; it was able to support dozens of telephone connections. During the time of low telephone penetration, HAX switchboards were popular in schools, hospitals and mines. The market was promising, and Ren Zhengfei earned Huawei's first earnings with these.

Since the HAX switchboards met customers' needs effectively, sales volumes stayed high as always. However, two years later, problems occurred after Huawei had taken customers' deposits. The problem was that the Hong Kong Hongnian Company couldn't supply enough goods at times. To protect Huawei's credentials in the business, Ren Zhengfei gritted his teeth and made the decision to assemble the small unit switchboards in two weedy warehouses in Shenzhen Gulf by importing components and hiring technicians.

No one could foresee that these electronic components and imported circuit boards, built by the hands of a dozen or so technicians, would be assembled to the specifications of a global enterprise.

CHAPTER

3

HARD WORKING

Our greatest glory is not in never falling,
but in rising every time we fall.
– Napoleon

Ren Zhengfei started his business in consignment sales and made his fortune by developing Huawei's own switchboards with independent intellectual property rights. Huawei's products, which are the tangible fruits in the blooming tree that is Huawei, pervade all types of telecom applications today.

Ren Zhengfei didn't rise to the rank of general during his many years of military service, but he commanded thousands of his soldiers in the business world, fighting towards his dreams in heroic leaps.

BUSINESS START-UP: LOCKING THE TARGET OF SPC SWITCH MACHINE

I will take fate by the throat.
– Beethoven

After the Third Plenary Session of the 11th Central Committee of the Communist Party of China put forward major policy decisions on reform and opening up in 1978, economic developments began to embark at a breakneck pace.

In the hot telecoms market, domestic telecom operators intended to introduce the advanced Stored Program Control (SPC) switch production line from abroad. But at that time, western countries limited the export of high-end technology to China. The production line couldn't be imported.

International telecom giants were sensitive to the market, and sent their strong sales troops to promote SPC switch products, which made an easy launch in the Chinese market. After a few years, the Chinese telecom market was shaped by eight companies from seven countries: NEC and Fujitsu of Japan, Lucent of America, Nortel of Canada, Ericsson of Sweden, Siemens of Germany, Bell of Belgium, and Alcatel of France.

At that time, Huawei was a little-known, small company. With rampant high-priced foreign SPC switch products, and a deluging assembly of smuggled SPC switch machines in the market, Ren Zhengfei told Huawei technicians: "We must develop and manufacture our own brand of SPC switch machine!" With his unyielding nature, Ren Zhengfei locked onto the target, a BH01 SPC switch machine with 24 connection ports to be produced.

The warehouse where the small unit switchboards were assembled could not meet the development needs of Huawei at that time. In September 1991, Ren Zhengfei took his fifty plus young employees to newly rented offices on the third floor of an industrial building in Haoye village, Bao'an county, Shenzhen, which became the new battlefield for Huawei to forge its own brand.

At that time, few enterprises owned by national telecom administration were manufacturing small SPC switch units with 34 and 49 connection ports. Ren Zhengfei bought the components from the state-owned companies, and started to assemble the Huawei brand 24 connection ports unit. The small SPC switch unit was a mature product and required little new technology. They just needed to weld separate components on the circuit board according to the cir cuit diagram.

The small BH01 SPC switch made by Huawei had relatively fewer connection ports and simple functions, which confined customer groups to hospitals, mines and other institutions with limited telecom needs.

When the small BH01 SPC switch unit entered the market, supply fell short of demand quickly because of its price advantage compared to other domestic products.

Huawei became an immediate hit. The large sales volume gave Ren Zhengfei another unforeseen cause for a headache: the short supply of separate components. To reverse the tough situation, Ren Zhengfei asked his employees to keep assembling products, and to research making SPC switch units at the same time.

Huawei's technicians had learned all there was to know about the small BH01 SPC switch – inside and out. They were able to use this knowledge and gradually designed the Huawei brand electric circuit with appropriate ownership rights, and developed exclusive software programs.

The purported factory and research and development (R&D) centres were simple, each right next to the other. New products developed by the R&D centre were sent to production in the factory immediately, to speed up the process of market launch.

To boost morale, Ren Zhengfei told the technical staff and assembly workers: "When you buy your house in the future, remember to choose one with a big balcony facing the south, where all the money that you will have made can bask in the sunshine. It may get mouldy otherwise."

Huawei's technicians were devoted to working untiringly: crouching over their work tables when tired, and continuing to work after a short nap. They would even work in the hot and humid Shenzhen summer with no air-conditioning, relying only on the ceiling fan over their heads.

To expedite the research and manufacture of the new product, Ren Zhengfei lived in the factory every day, and always proposed to treat everyone: "To have something good, let's make some pigtail soup tonight."

Despite difficult times, all Huewei's employees were happy when they squatted around a pot of pigtail soup, holding their bowls, nibbling pigtails and drinking the soup. Their tiredness would be gone. With Ren Zhengfei there with them, through thick and thin, they believed in the monumental development of Huawei in the future, and that they could make more money and have a better life.

Huawei's small-unit SPC switch development project team only had six people designing hardware and software. When faced with testing the performance of the new product, the question of how they could test the operations without any professional testing equipment arose. But Huawei's engineers were very smart and came up with the solution of manually inspecting each individual solder joint with magnifying glasses to ensure there was no weak welding or errors in nearly 10,000 solder joints. After that, they used multimetres to test each electric circuit. After all this, they still had the last operation to run: the large traffic test.

At that time, all Huawei staff would put down the work in hand, each holding two telephones, and dial at the same time, after counting down one, two, three. They then waited until connected and hung up at the same time. They used this method to test the processing capacity during large traffic, and Huawei's new machine met all quality standards in various tests.

Shortly afterwards, Huawei's equipment department team developed test equipment for large traffic, and quit the original manual method used for large volume traffic tests.

DIFFICULTIES TO BE CONQUERED

Learn extensively, inquire thoroughly, ponder prudently, discriminate clearly, and practise devotedly.
– Book of Rites

The launch of Huawei's BH03 SPC switch was timely. By then, Ren Zhengfei had spent every penny of his savings, deposits from customers and usurious loans for research and development. If they hadn't produced the first three, ten-thousand-count shipments of SPC switch machines, Huawei had no way but to go but towards bankruptcy.

The BH03 type switch unit provided a clear call connection and worked smoothly. Soon it earned the network license from the telecom department. The instruction manual for this new switch unit included the message: "Wish you success soon. Telecommunication is your catalyst, and an excellent small switch unit will make a difference for your office."

There was also a line of small print in the instructions: "Users' training workshops will be from the 10th to 18th each month in Shenzhen and repeated each month. No further notice will be given regarding this. The technical training is free of charge, the cost of living not included. Everyone is guaranteed equal treatment whether making orders or not."

Huawei not only made a great effort on developing SPC switches, but spent a lot of time on promotion among distributors and users after they made it.

Chen Kangning used to work in the Chongqing Telecommunication Bureau. In the tide of resignation and taking to business, he left the work unit and opened a small telecom company. Ren Zhengfei and Kangning met for the first time at the end of 1987, when Ren Zhengfei met with Kangning to expand the market. Kangning firmly recognized Ren Zhengfei's business philosophy. Soon after Ren Zhengfei returned to Shenzhen, he immediately sent the information material about Huawei's switch machine to Kangning.

On the back cover of Huawei's switchboard information materials there were two paragraphs: "go to the countryside, to rural regions, to accomplish in the vast land – this is the strategy of encircling the city in rural areas, the magic weapon Huawei adopted in its startup, which has been proven absolutely correct with time."

The second paragraph was even more touching for Kangning: "customers can return Huawei products in any condition, and remain as welcomed by Huawei as when they bought them."

Kangning started his business to make money, and he had been the agent for another brand. He was used to the practice that when a customer made a purchase of a brand, they would be greeted with smiles. But if they needed to return the product, the company would change their face, either blaming the customer for improper use, or by making different excuses for declining the return. This practice was the source of much pain to Kangning but when he read Huawei's generous commitment, he felt as though light beams were touching his heart. From then and with no other concerns or reservations, Kangning became Huawei's agent in Chongqing.

Nearly all the switch machines made by either Huawei or other producers were still early-stage products and failures occurred now and then. With each breakdown, customers would go to the product agent for help. Ren Zhengfei put himself in the agents' shoes. In addition to an adequate supply of spare parts, Huawei also gave their agents like Kangning extra switch machines, with which they could relieve the immediate needs of customers, and in turn winning them more time for maintenance.

Kangning could foresee a bright future for Huawei through Ren Zhengfei's business philosophy and thoughtful consideration for the agents. In 1998, Kangning met a big client, with the aim of convincing the client to order from Huawei. Kangning decided to take his client to Huawei's office in Shenzhen to seal the deal there. However, when there Kangning realized Huawei's reception office was not as luxurious as he had previously thought. Huawei's staff were busy as beavers though, answering phones, making orders or replying to customers' inquiries, non-stop.

Even though Kangning's client didn't have complete trust in Huawei beforehand, he was impressed by such a pragmatic approach to work by Huawei's staff and decided to order Huawei products right away.

After hearing Kangning had visited Huawei's office with a client, Ren Zhengfei quickly put aside all his work and sent the only car the company owned to take Kangning, the client and some Huawei staff members out to a restaurant for dinner. After the welcome feast, the car took Kangning and the client to their hotel while Ren Zhengfei walked home.

In 1989, Kangning took a regional telecom bureau director from Sichuan to explore Huawei in Shenzhen. Ren Zhengfei accompanied them all day long and talked to the guest until midnight. Even after three or four hours of sleep, he would still arrive at the hotel by 7 o'clock in the morning to accompany the guest for breakfast and discuss contract details.

Leaders heralded business characters and development. After dozens of meetings with Ren Zhengfei, Kangning decided to join Huawei and become involved in forging Huawei's future. He had been waiting for an opportunity like this, and finally he had it.

In March 1990, Kangning was paying a visit to the telecomm bureau director who had visited Huawei, and he caught the director yelling at a domestic switch producer through the phone. It turned out that the delivery of a switch unit the office had ordered was delayed, time and time again for various reasons.

Right away, Kangning made a comparison between Huawei's switch unit and the one that the director had ordered. This convinced the director to quickly cancel the original order and sign the contract with Kangning to order Huawei's switch.

On 1st April 1990, the telecom bureau director, Cheng Kang, came to Huawei with this order. After that, Kangning became the head of the marketing department, manufacturing department and corporate culture department respectively.

On the night of 31 December 1991, Ren Zhengfei ordered a buffet and celebrated the success of the development and market launch of the BH03 switch unit with all Huawei employees. People who attended the celebration still remember the scene of Ren Zhengfei standing on top of a carton box giving his pep talk: "If we don't fight for it, we can't survive. Forty working hours a week will only make ordinary labourers, not scientists or engineers, impossible to prompt the industrial upgrade. In twenty years, of the telecom giants dividing up the global market, one will be Huawei."

HEROES JOINING IN HUAWEI

To verify jade requires three days of full burn; to identify the type of wood requires seven years of sprouting.
– Bai Juyi

In 1992, the hottest market in China was real estate; the most lucrative business was real estate. According to incomplete statistics, at the end of 1992, a total of more than 12,000 real estate development companies were registered in China. This number was triple the number that existed in 1991. Countless millionaires and billionaires arose in the frenzy of investing in real estate, especially in Hainan Island.

To strike it rich, it was believed that real estate was the way – a popular saying known to all in Shenzhen at that time. However, Ren Zhengfei didn't get carried away with this obsession with real estate investment. He clearly recognized a harsh winter would impact the overheated market. Huawei wouldn't become involved in this irrational and overwhelming frenzy.

Ren Zhengfei's judgment of the real estate market was accurate and his prediction proved correct. After a quick outburst of real estate development, in June 1993, the central government decided on macro-economic regulation of economic conference.

The Party Central Committee and State Council also issued instructions on the current economic situation and macro-economic regulation. They took 16 measures to improve and strengthen macro-economic regulations. After that, the real estate market cooled down rapidly.

According to the Chinese business magnate, Pan Shiyi, the Gold Rush in Hainan was where he made his first million RMB through real estate speculations. When he went to the local government to verify the approval of a business project, he accessed the internal documents and stumbled across the fact that the per capita housing area in Haikou had reached over 50 square metres, while in Beijing housing per capita was only 7 square metres. Pan Shiyi realized huge turbulence was approaching Hainan's real estate market. He immediately broke up with his six partners and retreated back to Beijing. Talking about the thrilling situation, Pan Shiyi still felt a lingering fear.

While the domestic real estate market was a roller coaster ride, Ren Zhengfei set up a bigger goal in his heart: he wanted to introduce high-tech talent and develop a new model of SPC switch with full intellectual property.

But success was not yet achievable by Huawei with its simple factory, heavy workload, incomplete canteen and dormitory. When the lecturer of Huazhong University of Science and Technology, Guo Ping, came to visit, he was immediately fascinated by the passion and creativity of Huawei's staff.

Ren Zhengfei spotted Guo Ping's talents and tried to convince him to join Huawei by depicting the potential future success of Huawei with confidence. Guo Ping was attracted by Ren Zhengfei's genuineness. After serious discussions, Guo Ping recognized Ren Zhengfei as a far-sighted entrepreneur, and decided to join Huawei and root down in Shenzhen to prosper forth and grow.

Ren Zhengfei rejoiced at having acquired such a talent in Huawei. He immediately settled Guo Ping down in Shenzhen and appointed him as the project manager for the development of the HJD48, a PBX switch that could connect 48 users, the second intellectual property of Huawei.

At that time, with regards to hardware and software, Huawei's R&D team was not very sophisticated. They counted on their spirit to go as far as they could, having the main goal of getting through to prospective clients on the phone.

Ren Zhengfei proved his unique vision correct. After Guo Ping came to Huawei, he was put in charge of independent research and development. Guo Ping was truly a talent. He inspired the company's technical staff to work hard day and night, and made great advancements in the development of the new HJD48 PBX switch.

Guo Ping became well-known at Huazhong University of Science and Technology. Once he had worked at Huawei for a while, he soon predicted that the next century would be Huawei's world. He decided to recruit more technical talent and had his eyes locked on one of his classmates, Zheng Baoyong.

Baoyong had been focused on the field of optoelectronics in university, but he was no stranger to telecoms. Baoyong's entrepreneurship was kindled by the aggressive passion he saw in Ren Zhengfei and the great commitment of Huawei's employees. Baoyong left Beijing and came to Shenzhen.

Baoyong did not really expect that his dream research environment after postdoctoral studies, one which he had dreamt of to succeed in life, was actually waiting for him at Huawei.

Ren Zhengfei acted as the tour guide and presented Huawei's products to Baoyong at the same time. After the tour, Baoyong came forward to take Ren Zhengfei's hand, saying: "Mr Ren, I have decided to give up the doctoral degree and come to work for Huawei." Huawei's gates remained open to excellent talent, but Huawei was not a big company at that time. Ren Zhengfei also appreciated the easy-going and frank personality of Baoyong. Hearing that he intended to join his company, Ren Zhengfei replied with excitement: "Huawei is counting on you and Guo Ping in the future."

HARDSHIP, THE CORNERSTONE OF SUCCESS

**It is the talent that we need
urgently to govern the country.
– Sun Yat-sen**

The development of the HJD48 PBX switch was successful soon after Baoyong came on board. The technical breakthrough of connecting 48 users using one HJD48 PBX switch doubled the capacity made possible by similar products in the market, and the HJD48 PBX switch soon became a hit in the market for its high quality and competitive price.

After that, Baoyong continued to exert himself and fulfilled his mission to lead the research group in developing a series of switches with 100 ports, 200 ports, 400 ports and 500 ports, all of which filled the gaps in domestic markets.

The year 1992 was the year of harvest for Huawei. With the production of inexpensive user switches, Huawei's sales group raided all markets, and the good news kept arriving in succession. By the end of the year, the balance of overall production reached 100 million RMB, with a total profit of over 10 million RMB.

In the early 1990s, two types of disorders prevailed in the domestic switch market: the first happened in the large office switches. Foreign telecom giants knew that small national factories could not manufacture large office switches. They leveraged the price jointly, and deliberately created the illusion of products being out of stock. Domestic telecom operators were subjected to these high-priced exploits. Fixing maintenance and component issues was inconvenient when these multinational brand switches ran into failure. Faced with this type of malfunction, domestic telecom operators could not express their rage.

The disorder in the small users' switch was even more chaotic. According to incomplete statistics, there were over a hundred manufacturers with products in the market: some sold brands from Hong Kong or Taiwan on consignment; some ordered circuit boards and frame cases and assembled their own product, neither of which owned intellectual property rights. If for any reason the switchboard had problems, they could do nothing but wait for a technician to be sent by the original factories.

The HJD48 PBX switch model produced by Huawei had its own intellectual property and maintenance personnel in different places. Users were reassured, and the degree of user satisfaction was high. Its popularity was foreseeable. However, intensifying competition and decreasing profit was inevitable. After deliberate consideration, Ren Zhengfei decided to march to the crossbar central office switch market, and confront the international telecom giants who occupied this market.

At that time Huawei encountered the same situation as Pan Shiyi had faced in the Hainan real estate market. The heated market of SPC switches attracted many competitors, resulting in the oversupply of products. As the market collapsed, only those who had prepared were able to survive.

The first central office switch Huawei produced was the JK1000, an analogue switching system. Ren Zhengfei had not anticipated that this central office switch would cause him to experience failure.

MATTRESS: THE MIX OF LOVE AND HATE

You should focus on your career. Without inflection lens, sunlight could not focus and burn things.
– W. Somerset Maugham

Huawei's R&D team began with only five or six engineers who had just graduated from university. They simply did not understand the program-controlled switches. In order to adjust to the role more quickly, they had a book in one hand, while attempting to draw the circuit diagram with the other. After arduous research, they finally developed the series BH01, BH03 and HJD48 switches.

As Huawei developed, the number of research engineers grew from the initial five or six to a few dozen. The 'friend' who accompanied the engineers during their sleepless nights was the mattress.

As Huawei's research staff entered the company, they could go to the general office to get a mattress roll and a towel. The R&D team would roll up their mattresses and put them in the bottom of or under the desk. 'Mattress culture' is a precise and vivid description of the crisis awareness and hardworking spirit of Huawei.

It was not Huawei that forced employees to work over-time, but the R&D engineers had a drive to get the out-come early and make new developments. They often exert-ed themselves past midnight after a busy day.

At noon, when R&D engineers were drained, they would get out the mattress, spread it out on the floor, and take a short nap. After waking up reenergized, they would work through the afternoon and into the night, when they would take out the unique treasure of a Huawei engineer – a mattress again – to get some rest during the night. They did this because they considered it a waste of time to walk back to their dorms.

The internal journals of Huawei employees have many stories, such as the time when a supplier went to make a de-livery at noon to Huawei. He was exhausted and fell asleep on a foam board on the floor. On waking up, he found an-other person lying beside him. He greeted him and when looking closer, found out it was Ren Zhengfei.

Hu Xinyu was the man who put Huawei's mattress cul-ture into the spotlight of public discussion. Hu Xinyu was originally from Yibin, Sichuan, and joined Huawei's R&D group with a number of his classmates at the end of June 2005. In April 2006, Hu Xinyu was engaged in an impor-tant research project near completion. Heavy project tasks required him to work long hours. Two o'clock in the morn ing became his normal schedule. He would doze off on his mattress in the office when tired and start research imme-diately after waking up.

During this period, Hu Xinyu had some physical dis-comfort. He went to the hospital and was diagnosed with viral encephalitis. On 28 May the 25-year-old Huawei employee died from his illness.

Subsequently, a domestic business newspaper reported the 'Hu Xinyu incident' in an article with the inflammatory title of "No Longer Have to Work Overtime in Heaven". In this report, the journalist wrote: "We have to pay attention to this tragic story that a white-collar worker with an admirable job died of fatigue at work. He was so young and energetic, with a promising future ahead ..."

Huawei invited Hu's father to Shenzhen, and quickly decided to offer compensation for Hu Xinyu's death. Huawei spokesman, Fu Jun, then made a statement to the public that although the excessive time spent at work and Hu Xinyu's death did not correspond directly, there was some relevance between the two. The company leaders attached great importance to the handling of the matter, and revised the company's policy on working overtime. From then on anyone wishing to work after 10 pm needed to get approval, and sleeping in the company was not allowed.

Ren Zhengfei self-reflected in pain, and solemnly proposed to create the position of chief health and safety officer in order to further improve staff security and the occupational health of Huawei employees. This position was the first of its type among big enterprises in China.

The position of Huawei's first chief health and safety officer was taken by the then vice president, Ji Ping. The responsibility of the post was to draw people's attention to safety (even including traffic safety). Huawei had also set up a health guidance centre to standardize health regulations and illness prevention in food, water, the office environment and so on. It also provided health and psychological counselling, and promoted a balance between work and rest in order to cultivate an excellent corporate culture.

Ren Zhengfei responded to the public discussion on Huawei's mattress culture with his famous speech: 'Resources will be depleted. Only the culture will live on and on':

"In the early days, our R&D department started with five or six developers. In the absence of resources and favourable conditions, we adhered to the hard-working spirit inherited from the 'two bombs and one satellite' event. We modelled ourselves on dedicated and assiduous science and technology workers of the old generation, overcame hard situations with diligence and tackled key problems, throwing ourselves into scientific research, product development and validation, and equipment testing day in and day out ... We didn't have holidays or weekends; we couldn't tell day from night; we dozed off on the mattress and resumed work as soon as we woke up. This is the origin of the mattress culture in Huawei. The mat is used only for lunch breaks now, but the 'mattress culture' recorded the diligence and hard work of the early generation of Huawei's people and represents the treasured spiritual value we need to inherit ...

"Huawei started in China and competed with world-class business giants from developed countries, who had decades, or even nearly a century of experience, with dominant market shares and customer bases, and world-class management systems and operational experience.

"Huawei had no special background, and only scarce resources to rely on. Except the spirit of aspiration, open-mindedness and self-reliance, what could we count on? If we had more than that, it would be hard work, which helped us bridge the gap with our rivals.

"Whether in the past, the present or the future, we must continue to maintain the style of hard work. Conquering the overseas market was expected to be difficult for a Chinese high-tech enterprise. The significance would be extraordinary as well. Fortune would not fall into our laps. We needed to work for it. God helps those who help themselves."

In 1992, a dozen of Huawei's engineers forged a capable development team under the leadership of Zheng Baoyong. This team previously only had experience in users' analogue switch development. With the new task of office switch development, they reported the final research proposal to Ren Zhengfei after a collective discussion. Ren Zhengfei came on board with Zheng Baoyong's proposal of developing an analogue office switch because doing so was congruent with Huawei's current strength and advancement, and entailed minimal risk.

After the plan was confirmed, Huawei named the office switchboard JK1000. Zheng Baoyong presided over the overall development, Xu Wenwei was responsible for the hardware portion, and Wang Wensheng was responsible for the software. The three of them worked side by side. They teamed up like a twisted rope, and would not let go or give up until the successful launch of the JK1000 switch.

ESTABLISHING JOINT VENTURE WITH MAUBEC COMPANY

**Even mistakes of the wise man
can pile into mountains.
– Ancient African saying**

Huawei's first office switchboard, the JK1000, finally took shape successfully. However, analogue technology, though popular at first, soon became obsolete. Essentially, Huawei's R&D team had built a house on the sand, which was doomed to be in jeopardy.

Ren Zhengfei's mistake was failing to keep up with the times. At the time when digital switch technology had matured, analogue technology was on the edge of being outdated. So, regardless of its successful development, the JK1000 was destined to be rejected.

Digital technology would certainly put an end to analogue technology; magnetic tapes were being replaced by mp3s and mp4s, and videotapes were being taken over by CDs. Although Huawei engineers were aware of this, they mistakenly believed that the end of analogue had not yet arrived. Moreover, the JK1000 was a preliminary product. The team believed that it would not be too late to develop digital technology communications after this product had sold out.

At that time, only one person realized the imminence of the digital technology age, Cao Yi'an, an ordinary Huawei worker. Though his word didn't carry weight due to his position, he loved Huawei and never stopped trying to locate Ren Zhengfei to speak to him.

Ren Zhengfei was touched and convinced by Cao Yi'an's earnestness. Ren Zhengfei immediately instructed the R&D department that although they were developing analogue switches, they should not neglect the development of digital switches.

An old Chinese proverb states that to win the first game is essential to win all games. Huawei would not allow failures in the development of office switchboards. Huawei not only invested a huge amount in development funds, but also mobilized an elite development force. However, the long journey of R&D was overly ambitious and it 'burned' out money from Huawei's account.

Although the sales of SPC switches made some revenue, they could not make ends meet by spending more than they made. Ren Zhengfei had tried every means possible to gather the money allocated for other purposes, and secure loans with high interest to pay off every month. He even wanted to borrow more from usury, but they would not let him due to a fear of bankruptcy for Huawei.

At this time Ren Zhengfei was pulling his hair out, but good news came to Huawei's aid. Sun Yafang, an engineer, came to join Huawei with 2 million RMB in funds. Sun Ya-fang used to serve in the army. After transferring from the army, she became a division-level cadre in a government institution in Beijing. When Ren Zhengfei went to Beijing for some paper work, he met Sun Yafang by coincidence. He had little money at this time, but his strong and unyielding vibe impressed Sun Yafang, who could see Huawei's promising prospect in Ren Zhengfei.

BRAINS ARE BETTER THAN BRAWN

Sun Yafang had graduated from the University of Electronic Science and Technology, and had worked in the government telecom sector before joining Huawei. She was attracted by the passion and hardworking spirit of Huawei's employees, including Ren Zhengfei. After joining Huawei, she first served as the training manager, then Changsha office director, and then took charge of the marketing department before rising to the position of executive vice president in charge of marketing and human resources. In the re-election of board members in January 2011, Sun Yafang was elected as chairman of the board.

The 2 million RMB was like a 'timely rain' for Huawei. Some of this money was her personal savings, but a larger part of it was through a loan which she had taken out for this purpose. With her 2 million RMB, Sun Yafang offered Ren Zhengfei a solution that solved a lot of problems for the credit-deficient company.

To ensure the success of the development of the JK1000 switch, Huawei allocated all its funds to the R&D department, leaving the factory employees short of a salary for months. At this time, this large sum came into Huawei's account. The company's main leaders decided to discuss whether to direct the money continuously to the R&D department or to pay employees' salaries to fix the low morale at the company.

Huawei's executives had a long meeting, but Ren Zhengfei could not make a decision. While Ren Zhengfei was in hesitation, Sun Yafang stood up and decided for Ren Zhengfei: to pay employees' salaries first!

After employees received their long-delayed salaries, some internal problems were naturally resolved and their drive and passion for work picked up immensely. At the beginning of the establishment of Huawei, the standard monthly salary of new recruits was 1,000 yuan for undergraduates, 1,500 yuan for those with a master's degree, and 2,000 yuan for those with a PhD, except for specially recruited staff.

Former chief engineer of business and software department, Zhang Lihua, wrote in an article: My salary was 400 yuan back in school. After joining Huawei, the first month I got 1,500 yuan. In the second month, my salary rose to 2,600 yuan. I was very pleased with my salary increase every month, which increased to 6,000 yuan per month by the end of my first year as an employee. However, I didn't get all that money in hand. Every month, I only got half of that in cash, and the other half remained in the company's account. When payment was issued, there was no official pay stub to document your earnings. We lined up in front of the finance room. Everyone could only see their own salary. You could take notes and take half of it away.

But Huawei was still in financial difficulty. Ren Zhengfei decided to convert the other half of employees' salaries and bonuses into shares in the company, to stabilize morale and reassure the workers. This was the origin of the 'Company Share for Everyone' scheme in Huawei.

Later, during a discussion with employees, Ren Zhengfei said: "We are now like the Red Army on the Long March. When tramping over snow-capped mountains and trekking through the grassland, we couldn't pay for the food and money we took from folks, only to leave a note for reimbursement after the victory." The employees' salaries were converted into shares in the company. Ren Zhengfei kept his promise and each employee finally got rewarded in the long run. When an individual decided to leave Huawei, they could cash in their shares, which made thousands of millionaires.

But Huawei's shortage of liquid capital was still a problem for Ren Zhengfei. In order to solve this, Sun Yafang suggested building a joint venture together with the telecom bureaus. Once the JK1000 switch was developed, the premier customers would be telecom bureaus in different regions. In all these years, Huawei's sales department had been reaching individual users and lacked experience in dealing with telecom operators. If Huawei and the telecom bureaus established a joint venture company, which was the equivalent of a community of shared interests, it would speed up the expansion and take-over of markets exponentially.

Sun Yafang's idea was very creative. Soon afterwards Ren Zhengfei proceeded to drive this idea in different local telecom bureaus. With his plans and schemes, 17 provincial or municipal telecom bureau leaders eventually agreed to set up a joint venture with Huawei called Maubec.

Maubec was established with a total of 39 billion yuan investments from the 17 telecom bureaus and 50 billion yuan from Huawei itself. Huawei promised a profit return of 33% to the 17 telecom bureaus after the setup of Maubec.

Maubec provided important support services to Huawei. It served strategic means rather than financial ones. After the financing of Maubec, Ren Zhengfei had 39 million RMB in hand. This huge sum of money relieved his anxiety.

Once Ren Zhengfei had developed the policy of the joint venture company, the different telecom bureaus involved and Huawei collectively turned into a community of shared interests, rather than of competing businesses. The company business replaced direct sales from telecom bureaus, and the exclusive cooperation with Huawei prevented other competitors from entering the market. The long-term goal of market occupation objectives transcended the short-term goals.

By consistent efforts, Huawei cooperated with China Railcom Company and established another 27 joint ventures including Huawei North, Huawei Shenyang, Huawei Hebei, Huawei Shandong, and so on. By then, Huawei's arms had stretched all over the country.

The joint venture finally completed its successful mission in 1999. When it broke up, Huawei was a very mature business corporation in terms of both capital sufficiency and market occupation, and no longer needed this government-business model.

STRAIGHTEN YOUR BACK, EVEN IN TIMES OF FAILURE

Don't fear the long road as long as
you are on the right track.
– Anonymous

When the JK1000 switch was successfully developed in early 1993, the joint venture set up by Huawei and the telecom bureaus, Maubec, was officially established. Huawei had removed barriers in technology and the market at the same time. Huawei was ready, from its top management, to its basic operational unit, to fight in the market.

In May 1993, Ren Zhengfei personally presided over the meeting of marketing managers, where he announced: "The focus for a period of time in the future is to promote the JK1000 switch in the market on a large scale."

To fight the sales war, Ren Zhengfei stressed at a meeting that the director of each office should personally lead the promotion. Elite training personnel should be mobilized for promotion planning and product presentation, while capable technical staff from the R&D team should be dispatched to be involved in the promotion and demonstration of the product. This is why Ren Zhengfei gave priority to the development of the analogue switches, in consideration of what local telecom bureaus' budgets could afford.

In 1990, the fixed telephone penetration rate was only 1.1% in China, ranking 113th out of 185 countries worldwide. This position is where the United States ranked in the early 20th century. But the digital switch was expensive, and the general telecom bureaus could not afford such a high price given the economic development at the time.

However, despite the volubility of the telecom experts, they could not foresee that only a decade later, the Chinese national telephone penetration would reach 50%, rather than the predicted 5%. The rapid development of telecoms could be attributed to two reasons. One was China's exponential economic development and the corresponding improvement of people's standard of living. Their need to install telephones increased by unprecedented high numbers. The other reason was the huge advancement in communications technology. The technology for digital switches matured, superior both in function and cost, which meant the advantage of the JK1000 model was stripped off both in performance and in price.

YOUR RIVALRY DETERMINED THE LEVEL OF YOUR SUCCESS

When the Huawei JK1000 analogue switches entered the market, the multinational telecom giants didn't seem to take this rising company seriously – a company which had just reached ten million in sales revenue and wanted to take a share of the spoils.

Foreign, giant telecom companies were competitive in experience. They had deadly weapons waiting for later competitors. They proposed to the telecom bureaus the forward working plan of 'constructing the telecom network all in one step', which included an optical fibre network in the city, and even for signal transmissions in remote rural areas.

The construction of the optical fibre network was not their real purpose. Their real purpose was to sell the corresponding digital switch they had just developed.

In the rapid development of the domestic market, the need for more telephones to be installed was compelling, and many telecom bureau leaders in the developed provinces could no longer wait. The scheme that the multinational companies had outlined was too glamorous and fascinating for them.

With the lobbying of multinational telecom companies, the domestic telecom industry began to believe that the application of optical fibre cables and digital switches would build the national household telephone network in one step, and once and for all. Huawei's JK1000 analogue switch had just launched, and met this situation head on, sliding to the awkward situation of having no market.

Surely Huawei would not accept the brutal fate of dumping the product that they had invested so heavily in and experimented with for a year. Ren Zhengfei summoned all his capable troops from the technical and sales departments together for discussion, after which he made two decisions. First, to publish articles in Huawei's internal journal for its employees to identify the current phase of domestic telecom development. It stated that Huawei should proceed gradually and not bite off more than they could chew. To leap forward in one step was unpractical. Second, to reinforce promotion of the JK1000 switch and invite potential buyers in the telecom bureau to the Shenzhen headquarters for discussion seminars when necessary. The aim was to convince them that the right choice was gradual steps in the development of telecom networks and to use Huawei's analogue switch JK1000 for a few years before the transition to the digital switch.

After Ren Zhengfei laid out the plan, the technical staff and sales associates immediately sprang into action. Soon afterwards, the first group of users from the bureau of telecom came to Shenzhen, at the Huawei sales staff's sincere invitation, to participate in the technical seminars Ren Zhengfei had prepared.

At that time, Huawei was headquartered in the Nanshan Shenyi Industrial Building in Shenzhen, a long hour away from the city centre by bus. No one knew Huawei. The bus stop was Yilida station.

On the top of the Shenyi Industrial Building was the sign for Huawei, written in traditional Chinese, which could be mistaken as 'Chinese Bird' if not read carefully. Many employees in Huawei joked with each other: "We are from the Chinese bird company!"

An eye-catching scroll containing an inscription written by General Zhang Aiping (Chinese communist military leader) hung on the fifth floor in the building: "Is it not a delight after all to have friends come from afar?" It was said to have been acquired by a vice president in charge of finance, who was a relative of Zhang Aiping.

In the issue of September 1993, Huawei People published an article with the title, 'Is it not a delight after all to have friends come from afar?' – the rural telecom technology and market seminar took place in Huawei. Zhang Rongjun, the chief of the rural telecom department of the Shangqiu area, said: "We had some user switches in Shangqiu, but satisfactory, especially during thunder storms. I inspected Huawei's counter products these days and found them nearly perfect."

After a tour of Huawei, Zhang Rongjun continued: "Telecommunications is developing in our country. We may use digital transmissions in the future, but now we are using the simulate relay board. I do not know whether we can only change our boards to upgrade our product while also selling at a lower cost."

After listening to Zhang's concern, Ren Zhengfei immediately replied with humour: "A year or two years down the road, the components will be middle-aged in terms of their working cycle, which means they could be resold to other places at half price. Why not do that? Or then reassign them to under-developed locations within province borders through the rural telecom maintenance centres. According to the market forecast, the JK1000 switch will not be obsolete until the year 2000. About a third of Japan used crossbar switchboards at that time, and the same percentage in Britain too."

In the year of 1993, Huawei engineers from the installation team worked tirelessly against all the odds. They trekked north and south across China, to both banks of the Yellow River, and eventually sold a total of over 200 sets of JK1000 analogue switches. That year, they left footprints in the fishing villages along the seaside, in the desert plateaus, and in the foothills and mountainous regions. Endurance, a hardworking nature, won the praise and approval of users.

Ren Zhengfei once said: "To serve customers is the only reason for Huawei's survival. Customers' needs were the development of Huawei's original driving force ... To work for your passion, to dedicate to your purpose and to meet opportunities and challenges is such a chance and needs to be cherished. We need to do everything meticulously, whether big or small, to cultivate the realization of our long-term vision: the open mind, the responsibility and the empathy beyond personal gains and losses ... Everyone devoted to his or her career should strike forward bravely without hesitation, whether on the road of flowers or thorns."

Although Huawei employees sold more than 200 units of JK1000 switches, while the technology was still immature, the most serious problem was the power supply during thunderstorms. A few JK1000 machines caught fire while in use during thunderstorms, and almost burned the entire engine room. The ministry of post and telecoms issued a strict order at that time: two hours of interruption of telecom networks cost the bureau director his post. The serious incidents wrongly caused a few bureau directors close to Huawei to lose their jobs.

In the failure of the JK1000 switch, Ren Zhengfei recognized the importance of product quality. Without good quality, Huawei would not exist. Without good quality, Huawei would have no future.

The JK1000 switch died before reaching victory, and became a sacrifice in the business battle with multinational telecom companies due to factors in technological and market demand. Huawei had not won anything in this brief confrontation. Huawei's installation team brought telephones to remote rural areas, a sign of progress and prosperity. The high quality of service for the telephone installation won the trust of users and made a big market impact. In the users' eyes, the temporary problem with Huawei's product didn't write off their genuine service.

Since the promotion of JK1000 switches across the country, Huawei made efforts to put customer service into action. After years of endeavours, Huawei established the most comprehensive customer service system in China, opened 29 offices in different places, and set up technical support centres and spare parts centres. Good service and prompt response became the major reasons for customers to choose Huawei.

The failure of the JK1000 made the military grounded Ren Zhengfei deeply aware of his own shortcomings. From that point in time, Huawei's R&D departments reinforced the effort to collect and analyze competitors' products through a comprehensive market analysis. From the information gathered, Ren Zhengfei identified the competitors' advantages and disadvantages, which allowed Huawei to set a precise goal of technological innovation and a direction for the future.

CHAPTER 4

THE RISE OF HUAWEI

OF

HUAWEI

Those soldiers who are not willing to be
a general are not good soldiers.
– Napoleon

The taste of failure from the JK1000 switches did not stop
Ren Zhengfei, just as hardship did not stop the Red Army
from reaching North of Shaanxi during the Long March
(October 1934 – October 1935).

C&C08 was a digital technology-based office switch
with ten thousand ports. Its development at Huawei was led
by Li Yinan. When the C&C08 made its successful debut
in Pizhou, it marked Huawei's transition to urban markets.
The days of close quarter combat with multinational telecom giants had finally come.

C&C08, IT'S HARD TO LOVE YOU

**The greatest test of courage on earth is
to bear defeat without losing heart.
– Ingersoll**

The development process of the C&C08 could be described as arduous. When problems occurred with the hardware, research engineers immediately set to dealing with them. When the problems with the software ensued, finding a solution was a slower and more difficult process. The design was not finalized and this had a continuous detrimental effect on its production, and Ren Zhengfei was torn with anxiety.

The comparison between this public switch to user switch was like that between the torrential Yangtze River and its tributary stream. To explain it with another example, the public switch was the arteries while the user switch was the capillaries.

In terms of their users, the consumers of user switches were small institutions like government agencies, small enterprises and mines; the consumers of public switches were different telecom network operators. For instance, the operators of Haidian district in Beijing needed to satisfy at least a dozen thousand individual users, while institutions like mines and schools merely had a dozen, or at most a hundred, users. The price of the public switch was decided by the number of users, which meant that to sign the contract with one telecom operator brought a few dozen institution customers.

Ren Zhengfei had the keen vision of an entrepreneur, and was well aware of the public switches that Huawei needed to develop for further development.

Chief engineer Baoyong again took the responsibility for the development of the public switch. But he always had a serious look on his face with this role and his outgoing nature was burdened with pressure.

To invigorate the R&D team and achieve results, Huawei was recruiting from electronic technology colleges across the country. With fresh graduates joining the R&D team continuously, Zheng Baoyong had to spare some of his energy that he would have normally spent on research to organize orientation and training for the new graduates.

The new graduates didn't have any knowledge or even understand how the public switchboard worked, but they were not lacking in entrepreneurial passion and hardworking spirit. These young college students came to the melting pot of Huawei, and were inspired by the thriving corporate culture. They were each given a guidebook on program controlled switches by Zheng Baoyong, which had a red cover and became widely known as the 'Red Book'.

Using the Red Book, these young people learned theories while they were practising operations, and in the shortest time possible they became experts in the R&D department.

As well as instability and shortage of talent, the Shen-zhen Hukou (a permanent residence permit) was another problem that the engineers of Huawei had to deal with. As a private enterprise, Huawei was not valued by the local government. Only a few core staff were granted Shenzhen Hukou, while most employees had to go back to mainland China as they were only granted temporary residence per-mits. Due to tight schedules and heavy workloads, some-times they couldn't get the permit approved in time. In such situations, when there was a security guard spot check at midnight, if an employee was caught without a permit, they would be forced to serve labour duties in the Zhangmutou working site in Dongguan.

After Huawei grew bigger and stronger, a national lead-er once asked the president Sun Yafang: "Can you describe how you feel about Huawei's success in one or two sentenc-es?" Sun Yafang replied bluntly: "Crying without tears."

Back then Huawei's staff was in a state of crying without tears. Without any background or technology available, nor the right conditions for apt scientific research, all that they had to confront the multinational giants with was their in-ternal drive and courage. The technical barriers wouldn't have been too hard to cross, since in order to compete suc-cessfully all that Huawei needed was to develop counter products against its competitors. But after the last defeat, Ren Zhengfei realized that they needed to set their minds elsewhere for survival; he realized that they needed to set their minds on the world's most advanced digital switch. The digital switch Huawei wanted to, and was in the process of developing, was intended to be equipped with the best hardware and the most progressive software. If they could not develop this with the latest technology, it could potentially repeat the fate of the JK1000.

Young people were the driving force and wealth. Huawei's chief engineer Baoyong was only 29 years old, and the average age of his researchers was 25, with the youngest aged only 19.

Baoyong divided the digital switch development into two groups: one responsible for hardware, and the other responsible for software. A total of 300 research engineers were assigned into fifty sub-project teams. Everyone carried out their duty in an orderly and meticulous manner in different sectors of design, programming and development.

Engineers in charge of hardware design were often locked in discussions when they encountered technical problems, sometimes arguing with each other. After their debates, different electronic components always found their best place on the board.

Software groups were required to study the software programming and coordination of order and function. Software was developed one after the other following careful calculation which often ran late into the night. After that, the program connection, testing, reprogramming and submission were completed.

Ten years afterwards, when looking back at that time, a technical staff member who used to work in the hardware group recalled: "By pinching and scraping, the electric circuit board seemed a little bit unreliable. Who could imagine that this unreliable product would succeed at last?"

Ren Zhengfei originally planned to launch this ideal digital switch before the spring festival of 1993. To meet this timeline, he pushed the research engineers to produce the schematic diagram, he also arranged the CAD people to wire the product at the same time. Since the schematic diagram was in constant change, it always fell to the CAD engineers to receive the new version of the schematic while they had their work half complete, leaving them foaming at the mouths and bristled with rage.

Forced to design and work in these conditions, they could not predict whether the digital switch they produced would be of good quality. Could they make a debut with this unreliable product to the telecom operators? As they worked under strain, doubts and anxiety were bred and spread.

Meanwhile, Ren Zhengfei held faith in Huawei's first digital switch. As it was said: without the right title, the words would not make sense. A catchy and meaningful name was needed for the switch while it was in development.

The research staff were asked to suggest the names of the machine while they were engaged in its development. A few names were proposed but got rejected by Ren Zhengfei. When the last name, 'C&C08', was suggested, Ren Zhengfei's eyes brightened, and he said excitingly: "That's it."

C&C had three layers of meaning. First, it represented 'Country & City', a symbol for Huawei to conquer from the city to the countryside; second, it meant 'Computer & Communications', both encompassed in the new model of digital switch; third, it was 'China & Communications'. Those were the official explanations from Zheng Baoyong when he reported this to national leaders.

The role out of the C&C08 advanced digital switch experienced constant delays due to difficulty experienced in researching and applying the most advanced technology.

Research engineers were anxious, Zheng Baoyong was anxious, but the most anxious person was Ren Zhengfei.

While the design of C&C08 was still in development by Zheng Baoyong and his team, Ren Zhengfei had assigned a sales taskforce: to sell the C&C08 model switch in its infancy.

With no actual product, no design blueprint, and not even an instructions manual, the sales people only had the 'concept' of the C&C08 digital switch, but managed to find its first buyer – the Fotang bureau branch in Yiwu, Zhejiang.

The sales team had signed the contract with the Fotang telecom branch with clear agreement that they would launch the switch in Fotang by May or June 1993. After signing the contract, as the time of the launch approached, the Fotang bureau pressed for this launch agreement date with nonstop phone calls. Ren Zhengfei felt as if his heart was in the frying pan, quite uncomfortable, as you can imagine.

Indeed, Ren Zhengfei had set a high goal for the C&C08 switch machine. He wanted it to be the most advanced in the country and not in any way inferior to global standards.

High demand escalated difficulties at times, which resulted in delays in its production. Ren Zhengfei faced both internal and external pressures due to constant delays of the C&C08 public switchboard. His heart was torn with anxiety and he felt that he had aged ten years.

RISKY LAUNCH IN FOTANG

Only actions can make your value.
– John Ficht

In October 1993, under constant demands from the Fotang telecom bureau, Ren Zhengfei called Zheng Baoyong to his office and said: "We can't wait any more to launch the C&C08. The market will be gone if we make them wait any longer. We need to launch right away."

Zheng Baoyong explained: "Mr Ren, we haven't completed the test of the C&C08 yet."

To which Ren Zhengfei replied: "The current situation doesn't allow for a step by step test. I am afraid by the time all the tests are finished, the contract with the Fotang bureau will be lost."

Zheng Baoyong nodded his head and made a decision: "We will run the tests while making the launch at the same time."

Zheng Baoyong's concern made perfect sense as a responsible scientific researcher. Huawei's C&C08 couldn't enter the market before full tests were passed. The C&C08 public switch should not reach customers if there was the slightest chance of problems with it.

But Ren Zhengfei saw things very differently; he knew that the C&C08 was the product that would help Huawei take off. It was imperfect, but which baby has the perfect cry on his first attempt? He was not too concerned about potential problems. With the support of the backbone of Huawei's technical stuff, Zheng Baoyong could lead them to work successfully in the Fotang bureau. They could install and test the C&C08 at the same time. If they lost this, the Huawei company that Ren Zhengfei had built would collapse. His painstaking effort and investment would be wasted.

In the winter of 1993, Zheng Baoyong took the truck, with the not-fully-tested C&C08 switch to the Fotang bureau to start its installation. The first C&C08 public switch was transported to the operation room in the Fotang bureau. Zheng Baoyong fended off any chance of negligence and led the installation personally. Zheng Baoyong stayed there personally. He led the elite technical staff to carefully debug the switch, and the result was unexpectedly shocking. The telephone could not dial through. When connection was finally established, after many attempts, the C&C08 was very unstable: it would be cut off in the middle of a conversation. The number of lost calls was high, and disconnections and breakdowns happened frequently. All the problems that Zheng Baoyong had imagined were happening to this C&C08 switch.

In order to boost morale, Ren Zhengfei travelled all the way from Shenzhen to Yiwu, and visited the engineers in the front line in the Fotang operation room a few times. The calm glamour Ren Zhengfei radiated comforted and encouraged the engineers and encouraged them to keep working hard.

The installation at the first Fotang bureau branch took place in the winter, despite the fact that there was no heating equipment in the operation room and the room temperature frequently dropped to below zero degrees Celsius. When the installation engineers were freezing they would wear two jackets, breathe on their hands and they would stamp their feet to expel the cold while their feet stung, bitten by the frost.

Huawei's engineers worked through the day, and would nap on a piece of cardboard box or foam board on the cold floor when tired at night. They would resume their work regardless of how late it was in the night, to test this chaotic digital switch even in the dim midnight light.

The director of the Fotang bureau branch, Mr Ding, was also under great pressure to use the C&C08 digital switch. However, he was impressed by the passionate dedication of the Huawei workers and believed he hadn't chosen the wrong partner.

Mr Ding clearly remembered one evening when he came home and had dinner. After a nap, he found it had snowed outside. The snow, wrapped in the cold wind, piled higher and higher. Mr Ding became worried about their bureau office. He put on his coat, picked up a flashlight and went to work against snow and wind.

The windows and doors were shut in the office, the telecom equipment was working as usual, but he caught a beam of light coming from the C&C08 digital switch operation room. He opened the door, found a dozen engineers either standing, sitting or lying down, with their attention fixed on the test of the C&C08 machine.

The wind was raw and biting outside, and the cold damp air was piercing the room, but the enthusiasm of the Huawei engineers formed a ball of warm flames, touching Mr Ding's heart. Mr Ding's support facilitated the adjustment process, and he made many comments on the appearance of the supporting team, the installation and so on. Customers were god to Huawei engineers. They spared no effort to meet Mr Ding's requests and standards, which in turn won Mr Ding's respect.

After two months of tests and adjustments, the C&C08 finally worked on its own. Though some problems still occurred later, and technicians from Huawei needed to be called for maintenance, Mr Ding chose Huawei's product and supported the national brand unswervingly, which kept inspiring Huawei.

It wasn't until a few years later, when branch telecom bureaus across Yiwu switched to use the C&C08 digital switch, that the performance of the C&C08 switch became stable.

To celebrate, Mr Ding brought a bottle of his home brewed wine 'Qingchagun' to treat the Huawei installation engineers. In the ensuing evaluation, inspectors from the Yiwu bureau spoke highly of Huawei's C&C08 product: "We used to use the 1240 model from the Shanghai Bell company, who were said to have developed a 16-user board a long time ago, which hadn't launched yet. We couldn't believe your model came out so soon, with such advanced technology. You are well ahead of others in the industry."

Huawei's user terminal was equipped with a full menu in Chinese, mouse operation support and hot keys for help. The interface was clear and beautiful, as well as easy to learn and operate. This spared operators the trouble of training for a new switch and lowered the possibility of operational mistakes. Customers were fully aware of the software security, reliability and accuracy at billing. The design of the maintenance tests and traffic statistics were practical and rich with functions.

The success of the C&C08 digital switch instilled excitement in Huawei from the top of the company through to the bottom. Ren Zhengfei was excited, with all sorts of emotion welled up in his mind. Later he made the well-known speech, 'Toast to each other in victory; Rescue each other in desperation':

"We are in the battlefield of business, where the brutality and hardship are even more persistent and enduring, a natural testament and opportunity for marketing leaders and troops. Without their sweat and tears, we wouldn't have achieved the sales benchmark of 120,000 lines installed per month. We would like to congratulate all members of the marketing department on behalf of the company. In a number of markets across the country, provincial authorities accepted the C&C08 digital switch at a high percentage. The market is expected to rise by 10% in June, which is inseparable from the night and day toils of scientific research personnel, excellent management of production systems, and the efforts of all different departments in the company. I'd also like to express my deep gratitude to them on behalf of the marketing team."

There were still shortcomings and imperfections in the design of the C&C08, but users were discerning in their choice. The praise and testimonials given by the Yiwu bureau proved that the C&C08 digital switch was up to standard in the high technology market and met the needs of the Chinese telecom bureaus in call billing, traffic statistics and subsidiary operations. Although foreign brand switches were advanced and stable, the distance of geography and culture made them incapable of fulfilling the needs of Chinese customers.

Huawei took users' needs and concerns as the goal of its research and development, and responded promptly and thoroughly in after-sales services, which was the main reason for the popularity of the C&C08 switch in Chinese rural markets.

Ren Zhengfei was deeply aware of the fact that as a first generation product, the C&C08 digital switch was not beautiful in design nor stable in operation compared to the switches of multinational brands. He issued instructions to the R&D department that they needed to make further improvements based on user feedback, and outlined a higher-level version of the C&C08 for the future.

Afterwards, R&D hired the best designers from Germany to design the frame, rack and cabinet in order to improve the C&C08's appeal, and added news features to support remote users. After eight years of continuous optimization, new versions of the C&C08 began to dominate the market, and it became a world class switch that laid the foundation for Huawei's prevailing status.

In order to sell more of these digital switches, Zheng Baoyong would draw diagrams of the C&C08 to explain how it could be expanded to 128 modules, which was both a bragging and a promotional point. It signified that the features and the performance of the C&C08 were up to the advanced standards set by international markets. This was despite the fact that at that time even many of Huawei's technical staff could not understand how the modules worked. However, afterwards, the C&C08 fulfilled these functions and expanded to 128 modules.

It was later proven that Zheng Baoyong had not been bragging but had been outlining the blueprint for victory, even back then.

Ren Zhengfei made a summary of this history in Huawei's 'Current situation and our missions' brief:

"Zheng Baoyong started with a 40 port switch. He worked on the production of the switch as well as its installation. An outsider from the laser research field adventurously aimed at the most advanced switch model, better than the AT&T5, and got support from the idiot Ren Zhengfei. How much they were like a modern Don Quixote. After Zheng Baoyong took the successful C&C08 to an exhibit in Las Vegas, he gave me a call and said it was thrilling to look back. No one conducted research like we did across the world: adopting so many technologies with an equipment for reference, and settling all matters in one step. Fortunately, we succeeded. I couldn't imagine the consequences of failure."

IMPORTANT TALENT LI YINAN

**Talents are treasures of the country,
support of the state.
– Exaltation of the Virtuous by Mozi**

Li Yinan's name was inseparable from the C&C08 digital switch. It could be said the C&C08 made Li Yinan's name, and vice versa.

Li Yinan was born in Hunan in 1970 and was admitted to the junior program at Huazhong University of Science and Technology at the age of 15. He was legitimately an alumnus of Zheng Baoyong from the Huazhong University of Science and Technology. Huawei was a small company with hundreds of people back then. Though it had clear directions, Huawei was short of both a knock-out product and accurate market expectations. Young and talented, Li Yinan didn't prioritize Huawei in his career options. Like most of his classmates in the junior program, he intended to go abroad for further education, to lay a solid foundation and accumulate resources to start up his own company in the future.

Li Yinan came to intern at Huawei with no serious commitment to staying. However, when he joined this passionate group, just like a piece of steel that fell into the furnace, he felt his talent, his youth and his ambition were heated up in this small enterprise. He found the company to be extraordinary.

Ren Zhengfei had a saying that Huawei would never allow a moral model like Lei Feng (a legendary soldier of the Chinese army) to wear old socks in thrift, or let liver disease plague hard working people like Jiao Yulu (a devout and honest Chinese politician). The actual respect for talented people touched Li Yinan when he first heard of this. Ren Zhengfei said in a speech: "For compensation and benefit, the company would consistently lean to excellent staff to give a reasonable return to dedicated workers, so that the unassuming and humble people who devoted themselves to the company quietly could all get their share. As leaders of the company, we should not turn a blind eye to the less visible hard working staff. We should discover people like Lei Feng and treat them well, to create a corporate culture where those like Lei Feng won't get the short end of the stick. Only in this atmosphere, more people like Lei Feng would grow, and the corporate culture would be right and better, which in turn would facilitate business development."

Ren Zhengfei's broad foresight and distinguished philosophy to not overlook talented people impressed the young college student Li Yinan. He admired Ren Zhengfei.

The short internship brought Li Yinan's talent to the fore, which left a deep impression on Ren Zhengfei. As an intern, Li Yinan was entrusted by Ren Zhengfei to preside over a research project, and a set of laboratory equipment worth 200,000 USD was bought to meet that end. Huawei was not rich in financial resources at that time, and the investment of over one million RMB for an intern's project was a precarious risk, but Ren Zhengfei acted against the odds due to his trust in Li Yinan. Unfortunately, after the equipment was imported to Shenzhen, the project had to be aborted because of a sudden downturn in the market. There was no value to keep going. While Li Yinan was on pins and needles, Ren Zhengfei comforted him: "Working in technology development, it is common to run into a dead end. The most important part is to learn from the failures and start again."

Li Yinan's first option was to study abroad after graduation, but he had some problems with his visa application. Ren Zhengfei was eager to acknowledge and help talented people so Huawei contacted Li Yinan through his adviser at the Huazhong Science and Technology University where he had been studying. After much persuasion from Ren Zhengfei and Zheng Baoyong, Li Yinan abandoned his plan to study abroad and officially joined Huawei in 1992 at the age of 23.

Li Yinan was cultured and polite, and had the look of a delicate scholar. If he had not interned at Huawei in 1990 and got to know Ren Zhengfei's open mind and generosity, it would have been quite a challenge for Huawei to attract someone of Li Yinan's talent to join the company. On the other hand, if Li Yinan had enrolled on a doctorate programme, he would have found later that no other company would have gone to such great lengths in giving him a wonderful environment where he could succeed by virtue of his talent.

After only two days at Huawei, Li Yinan was officially promoted to the post of an engineer. Two weeks later, he solved a critical technical problem and the exception was made to promote him further to a senior engineer position. His brilliant work resulted in him being appointed as the deputy manager for the critical research centre only six months after he had joined Huawei. In only two years, he rose to the president of the research centre and chief engineer of Huawei. In four years, the 27-year-old Li Yinan became the youngest vice president of Huawei to take charge of research and development.

In addition to his aptitude in research and leadership, Li Yinan was perceptive and a visionary with regards to the trends of technology development. Huawei's staff commented in amazement: "Li Yinan's every move had an impact on Huawei's development direction."

The C&C08 with 2,000 ports was very successful in the market; Huawei's business was snowballing growth. Li Yinan and Zheng Baoyong were the right arm men of Ren Zhengfei. In order to take Huawei through another challenging leap, Ren Zhengfei issued the instruction to direct all the financial and research resources into researching a C&C08 with 10,000 ports.

However, Huawei was shy of engineers for the development of the C&C08 with 10,000 ports. Ren Zhengfei immediately asked the hiring department to "bring the best technical staff to Huawei!"

As for hiring, Ren Zhengfei had an interesting conversation with the human resources staff when they consulted on the standard of hiring. Ren Zhengfei asked them: "If Deng Xiaopeng [a Chinese revolutionary and statesman] applied, should we hire him?"

Some replied yes while some replied no. In fact, Ren Zhengfei had the answer in his mind: enterprises needed to consider which tasks people were best suited for. They could hire Deng Xiaopeng, but the first concern was to understand what he would be suited for.

With instructions from Ren Zhengfei, Huawei gradually developed systems and strategies for attracting and hiring excellent staff for the right roles. They pursued talented people regardless of the occasion and situation.

When the National Telecom Ministry organized a training workshop for program-controlled switches in Xi'an, Ren Zhengfei informed the hiring department and requested them to send the best technical staff to enroll in this training workshop.

Huawei's recruiters came to Xi'an. They learned at the workshop during the day, and went to make friends by visiting each dormitory at night. In fact, they were lobbying for recruitment. A senior technician from the Changchun Telecom Equipment Factory, Mao Shengjiang, was hired by Huawei at that conference.

For 13 years, while working at Huawei, Mao Shengjiang was responsible for research and development, production and marketing, and served the position of R&D department manager, vice president of the marketing department and senior president of Huawei. He spearheaded many brilliant achievements developed by Huawei's development staff.

Xu Wenwei was hired from another company too. Xu Wenwei used to work for a big foreign company in Nanshan, Shenzhen, whose office building bordered on Huawei's. After Xu Wenwei went to Huawei, his former employer was furious and managed to get the police to detain him at the police station through his connections. It took Ren Zhengfei a great deal of effort to get Xu Wenwei out of the police station.

A lot of Huawei's staff were scouted from the Telecom Research Institution. During each spring festival break, Ren Zhengfei assigned tasks to Huawei employees who went home for the holiday: "As you enjoy the spring festival at home, please find and recommend a few of your former colleagues or classmates to Huawei."

He also set up a Talent Recommendation Award for those who succeeded.

Another method of recruitment was to organize career fairs in colleges and universities, including the Beijing University of Posts and Telecommunications, Huazhong University of Science and Technology, University of Science and Technology, and so on. All of these became talent bases for Huawei.

Ren Zhengfei respected talented people, appointed them by merit, and awarded great compensation and benefits for their contributions. He also created environments and conditions for them to win various awards and facilitated their rise to the top, allowing them to become experts in their respective fields.

Huawei always had a craving for talented people. In 1998 the Minister of Education at that time heard the claim that Huawei had the monopoly on talent and asked his subordinate to submit a list of college students hired by Huawei that year. After he read the long list of names in turn, he noticed that one fifth of the top-20 university graduates from national computer science and telecom programmes went to work for Huawei. It could be seen how Huawei's talent recruitment frightened its competitors.

In 1997, Zheng Baoyong won the fifth China Youth of Science and Technology Award, the top prize of its category in China. In 2002, Liu Ping won the First-Grade Award for Progress in Science and Technology in Guangdong and met with national leaders. These awards typically took scientific workers dozens of years of work to achieve, but Zheng Baoyong and Liu Ping managed to receive these in their thirties. Huawei helped them achieve the dreams many scientific workers devoted their lives to and, in doing so, Huawei touched them in their hearts.

Ren Zhengfei never entered any award competition personally. He was indifferent to fame and wealth, he left that for the young people in Huawei.

DEVELOP THE DIGITAL WITH 10,000 PORTS

Appoint people by their merit.
– Zhu Yuanzhang Analects

The launch of Huawei's C&C08 2,000 port switch struck the market. This honorary product broke the technology and market monopoly of foreign brands and outmanoeuvered domestic competitors like Julong and Datang. Using a strategy of encircling cities from the countryside, Huawei continuously encroached on the market share of multinational companies and became the leading brand in the domestic telecom industry.

People were prone to jump to conclusions about Huawei's achievements, believing that the success of Huawei belonged to an emphasis on research and development. No matter developed by which telecom provider, the first developed C&C08 2,000 port switch became a hit in the market, and the company would scale the heights of industry.

In fact, Huawei was not the first to develop the 2,000 port switch or the later 10,000 port switch. At the beginning of 1993, Huawei mobilized all R&D resources to the development of the C&C08 2,000 port switch, when Zheng Baoyong asked Li Yinan and some other staff to plan for the development of the switch with 10,000 ports. The plan was discussed back and forth and could not be settled. In fact, the engineers were not in a rush at this time because of the huge market success of the C&C08 2,000 port switch.

To boost morale, Zheng Baoyong patted his chest and said: "You have the task of developing it. Once it comes out, I guarantee I will sell eight or ten units."

Ren Zhengfei had a sensitive insight. He found Zheng Baoyong not only capable in research and development, but also effective in leadership and management. He promoted Zheng Baoyong to the position of president of the central research department for the first term, which presided over the branch departments of switchboard business, smart gadget business, new business and basic business.

Among the four branch departments, the biggest was the switchboard business department, where Li Yinan was the manager; after all, Huawei was developing various business pillars. Once the switchboard market was saturated, Huawei would transfer focus to the new fields of mobile communication, optical fibre transmission, data communication and so on.

The development of the 10,000 port switch was more complicated than that of the 2,000 port switch. Even with his exceptional talent, Li Yinan could not complete the project independently. At the very beginning, he recruited Liu Ping and Yu Houlin. Liu Ping was responsible for the software development while Yu Houlin was responsible for the hardware. Liu Ping and Yu Houlin were almost the same age, and both were experienced engineers from a research institute in Wuhan. Their partnership was a perfect and effective combination.

Aware of the hard work that the research engineers would be engaged in, Ren Zhengfei asked the canteen staff to prepare various dishes and late night snacks to provide fuel for the researchers' bodies and minds. He would also go to the switchboard development department to talk to research staff for encouragement.

Li Yinan and Zheng Baoyong were the core force behind the development of the 10,000 port switch. The C&C08 port switch with a 10,000 capacity of ports was an upgraded version of the C&C08 with 2,000 ports. With regard to how to connect different modules, a bold idea occurred in both of their minds – the application of optical fibres.

In the early 1990s, optical fibre transmission was not yet a mature technology. Even the most advanced military operations of the time didn't use optical fibre transmissions and didn't even have an optical fibre network in development, let alone a private company like Huawei. After careful deliberation, Li Yinan proposed a plan to apply Synchronous Digital Hierarchy (SDH) technology, a relatively matured optical fibre technology.

The hardware design was carried out intensely in an office in the R&D department. Yu Houlin and a few other engineers completed the model of optical transmission analogue circuits and patterns. However, the switch board developed in the C&C08 was like a huge antenna, and it received disturbing signals and disabling optical transmission. After a few weeks of contemplation, as well as help from the logic analyzing inspector valued at one million RMB, the problem was finally solved.

Liu Ping's software development was not going smoothly either. The system software in the C&C08 10,000 could be divided into three categories, namely operation software, supporting software and program software. The algorithm was complicated and no shred of error was tolerated. The design reserved the upgrading space and encompassed the remote control and automatic billing system as well. All these systems needed to be more convenient and advanced in practice and operation than those of the C&C08 2,000 port switch. With the encroaching deadline, Huawei engineers needed to build the board for experiments and to test it right after the circuit design came out, and if it worked, send the diagram to Hong Kong for immediate manufacturing at double the price.

In the final stages of connection and adjustment, the research engineers became a bundle of nerves, for the fear of a small error on their part would hinder the project.

After two years of goal-oriented development, the C&C08 10,000 port switch model was developed in 1995. Looking at the model they had worked so hard to develop, tears welled up in some engineers' eyes.

On the day of joint tests, Li Yinan led the hardware and software teams. After a deep breath, he picked up a telephone connected to one module and dialled. Another telephone connected by another module rang.

Liu Ping picked up the other telephone and answered: "There's a connection!"

Just as Liu Ping spoke, Li Yinan cut in, before the applause of a victory celebration from all the engineers, "Did we set it in the permanent connection in the trial?"

Liu Ping hurried to check, only to find out that it was set in the permanent connection. This invalidated the connection that was just made. After revoking the permanent connection, the telephone became mute and they couldn't get through any more.

A faux connection elicited a flash in the pan. The hardware and software teams hustled to look into the reason and finally pinned the problem on the connection between software and hardware where the joint integration was not done well. After clearing up the problem, the telephone got through and, with the ring, a smile finally crawled onto Li Yinan's face.

On hearing of the successful test of the C&C08 10,000 port switch, Ren Zhengfei abandoned the work in his hands and hurried to the operation room. When he saw for himself that it had finally become a real product, he was thrilled and said: "I will arrange a big celebration for you!"

The guests at the celebration could not have got enough wine during the party. But, while Ren Zhengfei was toasting different Huawei staff, another serious problem struck his mind: Did the 10,000 port switch need to be thunder proof?

It was a recurring problem in the domestic telecom industry. The advanced foreign telecom companies could not foresee the problem after they entered Chinese markets. The user board was subject to interference or damage by strong currents experienced during thunder and lightning, and this even caused major accidents with switches burning.

After Ren Zhengfei's instructions, the then vice president Zheng Baoyong was responsible for this challenging task. To complete the mission quickly, Zheng Baoyong took command.

Huawei's engineers conducted a literature search and simulated experiments on the causes of dysfunctions in fuses when experiencing high voltage and proposed a few protection plans. To verify the efficiency of the protection plans, Zheng Baoyong moved the research team to the Guangdong Provincial Telecom Research Institute and conducted the tests together with the institution's experts, and finally came out with an effective plan. After 15 days of hurried manufacture, the first national thunder and lightning protector was invented by Huawei.

After they had developed their most competitive product, the C&C08 with 10,000 ports, Huawei's huge sales force initiated an overwhelming fearless charge into the market, which at that time was mainly dominated by foreign digital switch brands.

PIZHOU, THE STARTING POINT TO TAKE OFF

Adversity reveals genius,
fortune conceals it.
– Horace

If the launch of the 2,000 port digital switch was like a high school entrance examination, then the launch of the 10,000 port digital switch could be compared to a college entrance examination. Huawei passed this exam, and gained a firm foothold in the telecom market in small cities and counties.

The development gap between cities and the countryside was huge. The digital switch market in cities was shaped by eight foreign companies from seven countries. However, no telecom bureaus were willing to give products produced by domestic brands a shot, even if they were much cheaper than the foreign models. It was an implicit rule for the employees responsible for buying equipment in telecom bureaus: buying foreign brands was accepted, while buying an unstable domestic brand would cost them their job if any problems occurred.

The Pizhou Telecom Bureau had purchased a batch of S1240 digital switches from Bell in Shanghai a few years ago. As the demand for telephone installation increased with economic development, the capacity of these switches was challenged. The Pizhou Telecom Bureau decided to order another batch from Bell. However, the ordering agent brought back disappointing news that orders for Bell switches had already been scheduled for the next year – that they would not be able to take on any more orders.

Huawei's Nanjing office director, Xu Xubo, heard this news and immediately reported it to Ren Zhengfei. Ren Zhengfei recognized this invaluable opportunity and instructed the Nanjing office to take this order at any cost. With Ren Zhengfei's high hopes, Xu Xubo and a sales associate, Yang Jun, knocked on the door of the Pizhou Telecom Bureau. With earnest words and good intentions, as well as a detailed comparison of the product quality, functions and price between the two brands, they finally kindled the interest of the head officer at the Pizhou Telecom Bureau for the newly developed Huawei switch.

Ren Zhengfei attached great importance to this launch, and sent his best troops to handle the installation. The line-up outweighed the launch of the C&C08 2,000 port model because the rival competitor was the well-known Shanghai Bell company.

Shanghai Bell was the first joint venture in the high-tech industry with foreign investment and the flagship company of Alcatel Lucent. The former, a well-established multinational corporation was headquartered in Paris, France.

Li Yinan and Liu Ping went to direct the installation personally. Huawei engineers started to fix the cabinet and connect the wires. After a while, a C&C08 switch with 10,000 lines was installed.

With eyes on the installed switch, Li Yinan waved his hand to say: "Start to test and adjust!"

The adjustment went smoothly in the beginning but then ran into a problem; they couldn't place a long-distance call to the upper level bureau in Xuzhou.

Before this C&C08 switch with 10,000 lines had left the factory, it had undergone a careful inspection as instructed by Ren Zhengfei. No such serious problems had taken place at that time. Li Yinan assumed the relay interface board had malfunctioned in transportation and called Shenzhen to send a new relay interface board immediately.

After the new relay interface board was installed, the problem remained. "What happened?" Installation engineers stared at each other blankly. Li Yinan pointed to the wire connecting the relay interface board and said: "Change the wire to see if that works."

Two engineers hopped into a taxi and rushed to Xuzhou. The relay line was not a high-tech product and could be purchased in most relatively big cities. What left them open-mouthed was that the replacement of the new relay line didn't allow the signal to get through either.

Li Yinan reported the situation to Ren Zhengfei on the phone. Ren Zhengfei was very sombre upon hearing about the unsuccessful first launch, and sent hardware engineers to Pizhou, group after group. Li Yinan stayed a whole week in the operation room, and still the supporting engineer groups sent by Huawei could not fix the problem of making distance calls by any means. Hardware team leader

Yu Houlin was extremely anxious as he took responsibility for the hardware issues. The first launch of the machine in Pizhou had no options but to be a success, at any cost. He examined each board, tested each line and didn't let any single solder joint or connecting port escape his attention. He repeated these mechanic investigations time and time again, after which he reconfirmed his belief that there was no problem in the hardware.

The C&C08 10,000 port machine didn't have problems with its hardware. Could it be in the cabinet? He looked down at the cabinet and shouted in excitement: "I found the reason!"

Hearing the cheer, Li Yinan and Liu Ping rushed into the operation room and found the simple reason for paralyzing the long distance calls. It was too simple to notice – the false connection of the ground line. Yu Houlin got out a wrench and tightened the screw of the ground line. The problem of making long distance calls was fixed immediately.

Li Yinan led a team of installation engineers to work for seven days straight, and still hadn't finished the adjustment of the machine. Some staff in the Pizhou Telecom Bureau became suspicious of the switch with 10,000 lines' function. Faced with rumours in the wind, Li Yinan and other people didn't explain anything. They believed the facts would speak for themselves. To speed up the adjustment and make a successful launch was the best reply to all of their questions. The course to happiness didn't run smoothly. After the hardware problem was fixed, the software ran into yet another massive problem.

The software problem didn't originate from the design defect, but from the rushed actions taken by the Pizhou Telecom Bureau. Staff at the Pizhou bureau were eager to recover costs and released telephone numbers before purchasing the Huawei switch.

According to the set procedures, telephones numbers should only be released after the installation and adjustment of the C&C08 10,000 switch, but the switch now needed to work before the adjustments could be made. The time slots were occupied, not allowing the switch to work at full capacity.

New programming would fix this problem, but time would not allow it. After meetings and discussions, Liu Ping adopted a bold temporary solution: to set up a software restart at 2am, which would release all time slots.

It was an act of expediency, and couldn't solve the problem at the core. Since no one made calls at 2 o'clock in the morning, it was the perfect time for the switch programs to restart. If someone was using the telephone then, they would get disconnected or couldn't get through in the first place. This practice was continued for over half a year. The issue of time slot releases was finally fixed after multiple software upgrades.

In the final stage of project acceptance, Ren Zhengfei and Zheng Baoyong flew from Shenzhen to Pizhou. After a huge celebration, Ren Zhengfei could not contain his excitement. He made an impassioned claim: "In ten years, a tripartite division will appear for Huawei, AT&T and Alcatel. Huawei will consume a third of the market."

At that time, Shanghai Bell had a long-time hegemony in the domestic telecom market, while AT&T dominated the world market. Everyone laughed at this comment, considering it a leader's boast. The future development of Huawei would prove it was not a boast, but a blueprint Ren Zhengfei outlined with his foresight.

Huawei kept up the momentum and launched in other places. The arrangement of the C&C08 switch launches was ensued by expert evaluation conferences, to which Ren Zhengfei attached a great importance for the sake of network licenses. He found a big room to evaluate the C&C08s, and borrowed a dozen analogue devices from all over the country for comparison. Ren Zhengfei said proudly: "We brought all the analogue devices in the country here."

The vice chief engineer, Liu Ping, led the preparation for the evaluation test, and the leader of the expert evaluation team was a professor from Beijing University of Posts and Telecommunications. The first part was the test for functions, which the C&C08 passed easily. When it came to the software test, it encountered some twists and turns. In order to provide the software engineers with more time if any problems arose that needed fixing, Ren Zhengfei had arranged for a reception where Huawei employees would take experts out for sightseeing or meals.

After being modified a few times, the software passed the test. But before Ren Zhengfei could take a rest, problems occurred one after another in the following test of property. These were confined by the hardware's processing ability and could not be fixed in a short time. Liu Ping reported this to Li Yinan immediately. Li Yinan gave him an idea, that is, to connect the calling party and called party in the same module, and make some connections permanent. Experts were experts, but they would have turned a blind eye to Liu Ping's manoeuvre, probably because his company was a national brand. The C&C08 passed the property test as well.

The evaluation experts commented on the report that, "The C&C08 switch with a capacity of 10,000 lines has reached an advanced international standard." Such an affirmation was a big encouragement for Huawei. The tests finally came to a successful conclusion. The problems that occurred were fixed by Huawei's engineers later.

Huawei moved forward with combined efforts in research and marketing and the C&C08 switch with 10,000 lines finally became a mainstream product in the domestic market.

In 1995, Lucent, a divestiture of AT&T, merged with Alcatel, and became Shanghai Bell-Alcatel, because of the competition with Huawei and other Chinese companies.

WOLF CULTURE: CHARGING FORWARD

There is no prey that you can't get, if you have ambition; There is nothing that you can't achieve, with the same ambition.
– Wolf Totem

Ren Zhengfei once said: "The development of enterprise needs a lot of people that are like wolves, with three distinctive characteristics: first, acute sense; second, unyielding aggressiveness; third, awareness of teamwork."

The core of the wolf culture of Huawei consisted of four words: 'greedy', 'wild', 'ferocious', and 'resilient'. In the recruitment of talent, Huawei was 'greedy'.

Liu Ping joined Huawei in 1993 as a senior software engineer, and was promoted to chief of the Beijing Research Institute due to his excellent work. There he was in charge of the development of data telecom products. At that time, data products development was an unprofitable project, but it was Ren Zhengfei's strategic preparation for the future.

The Beijing Research Institute was located in the China University of Geosciences, the office had been remodelled from hotel rooms with very dim lighting. Two or three people had to share an office with these rough conditions. But Liu Ping hired a cook to provide lunch for their researchers during working hours. With no room for a dining table or chairs, they just ate their meals in the corridor. To improve this situation, Ren Zhengfei invested 10 million yuan to buy a six-storied house and renovated it into a decent office for the Beijing Research Institute.

Ren Zhengfei came to inspect the Beijing Research Institute while on a business trip. When he saw the scarce number of researchers in the institute, he asked Liu Ping: "Why do you have so few people here? Haven't I told you to recruit more people?"

Liu Ping responded deliberately: "Mr Ren, we have not decided on the data communication products. There is nothing for more people to do."

Ren Zhengfei responded: "Do what I told you to. If there is nothing to do, have them sift the sand."

Liu Ping didn't totally understand Ren Zhengfei's thoughts, but he executed his commands. An important part of Liu Ping's work in Beijing was to recruit more talent at all costs. The new employees had nothing to do, so they set up a protocol software department that later developed the protocol stack, the platform of Huawei's digital products and the foundation of Huawei's later take-off.

In normal R&D operations, new digital switches needed to go through complicated tests and their problems completely fixed before leaving the factory. In Huawei, however, neither the C&C08 with 2,000 lines nor the C&C08 with 10,000 lines, were launched before the final revision. Huawei hurled the products at business opportunities, seized the market and adjusted during installation. But the 'wild' character of Huawei's R&D department won time and markets for Huawei. This 'wild' fast attack of the wolf caught its prey. When opponents started to react, Huawei had already taken the market. At that stage, it became even more difficult for Huawei's competitors to turn the situation around!

The development of Huawei was brutal. It was silent for the first ten years and amazed the world for the next ten. As the number of staff increased, Ren Zhengfei set up the system of "Company Shares for Everyone". In Huawei, the more company shares you owned, the more assiduously you would work. This was way more effective than tedious and implausible rules and regulations.

Huawei had to be 'ferocious' to survive – ferocious in the market, ferocious with its competition, and ferocious in combat.

German military theorist Clausewitz said: "War therefore is an act of violence to compel our opponent to fulfill our will." Ren Zhengfei understood this from his time in the military. It applied to business as well. When Huawei first entered the market, it didn't have the reputation that it does today and it was privately owned. It steered clear from the main force of its enemies and struck at its weak points in the vast, rural areas, to put strong forces in the rival's weak area.

Huawei used the 'human wave attack' to take on one telecom bureau after another. Multinational companies usually had three or four people in charge of each province's business. Domestic manufacturers usually sent one or two people to the county-level market. However, in the conquest of rural markets, Huawei assigned seven or eight sales associates to each county.

In 1996, the Ministry of Information Industry and the Ministry of Posts and Telecommunications held a procurement conference in Beijing. The major provincial and municipal officials and industry heads were in attendance. Huawei was prepared for combat, to win the installation market share for the next year. When the conference started, Ren Zhengfei issued a call for 'soldiers': officer directors, project managers, high level executives. Together with 400 elite sales associates, they went to Beijing in a formidable array. Only about 40 officials attended the meeting. Huawei sent out 10 times as many staff to make sure there was full coverage of major officials and telecom bureau heads.

Although Shanghai Bell and Qingdao Lucent both attended this conference too, they had not prepared as well in their personnel or exhibitions. They failed against the human wave attack from Huawei, who successfully received stacks of orders, exceeding the original goals they had set out to achieve.

Huawei's stories of wolf culture to 'impress clients and get contracts' were beyond comparison.

At that time, the domestic telecom market was still dominated by eight brands from seven countries. The Tianjin telecom market was mostly in the hands of NEC, a Japanese company. NEC invested in a joint venture together with the Tianjin city government, and the dominant position was unshakeable. Huawei sales staff took stock and decided not to fight face to face with NEC, but to take a detour. Using an opportunity presented by a campus telephone installation, Huawei looped around and ripped off a piece of the NEC telecommunications network.

Telephone installation cost a thousand dollars at that time, and the waiting time could be up to a month. Huawei developed a system based on the functions of NEC switches, and made it possible to install a telephone in each dorm of Tianjin University. This bold attempt didn't have a model to follow, and didn't sound reliable.

The NEC Tianjin branch were not happy with this 'imaginative' system, and they turned down Huawei's proposal for cooperation. Huawei took the bull by the horns, and installed this system at their own expense. When the system came into operation, the telecom bureau responsible for Tianjin University surprisingly rose to the top in revenue. The increasing phone bills reached almost 1 million RMB. The revenue earned from installing telephones in student dorms was ten times that of regular cases. Telecom operators in Tianjin were shocked.

This again showed Huawei's ferocious side. Telecom operators responded to this success immediately. All telecom bureaus with universities in their jurisdictions called Huawei for this business. They hoped Huawei could create another miracle of one million RMB in monthly revenue.

NEC responded passively and lost opportunities. Siemens held the Beijing market but the Beijing telecom bureaus approached Huawei and asked for their campus telephone service. This was a huge turnaround for Huawei, because campus telephone systems served as the leverage for Huawei to open the Beijing market, and the media showered Huawei with praise: "a small card opened a new world".

In May 2008, the Ministry of Industry and Information Technology, the National Development and Reform Commission, and the Ministry of Finance jointly issued notice on deepening telecom systems reform, the introduction of telecom restructuring. The reorganized China Telecom planned to invest 80 billion RMB to build up code division multiple access (CDMA) in the future, and called for bids worth 15 billion yuan that year in the sector of service networks and core networks.

The news lit up global telecom equipment suppliers. It was a feast for the capable. Ren Zhengfei immediately called a meeting with Huawei's high executives, where he stressed the importance of CDMA to China Telecom, and he said forcefully: "We need to get the biggest order at any cost!"

BEI CULTURE, TO USE BRAWN AND BRAIN

Merchants seek nothing but profit;
businessmen have the standard to do something,
but not others; entrepreneurs have the social
responsibility, to create value and
improve the society.
– Ma Yun

Wolf culture emphasized aggressiveness; Bei culture wisdom. Using the brain and brawn was a basic requirement for entrepreneurs. Huawei's sales staff had given full play to aggressiveness. As they took big orders one after another, Huawei was way ahead of its opponents.

The China Telecom CDMA bidding results for service networks was released: ZTE won 50% of the market share, followed by Alcatel-Lucent with 20%; the rest was divided between Huawei and Asiainfo-Linkage.

Core network services included switches and wireless equipment, where the real profit was. ZTE, Alcatel-Lucent, Huawei, Motorola, Samsung, Nortel, six major equipment suppliers gathered in the capital city. A fight for life or death was on the stage.

The China Telecom CDMA Bidders' Conference was held on 14 August 2008, at the Beijing Tangshan Holiday Conference Center. Huawei and five other telecom tycoons took part in this wireless equipment bid.

Alcatel-Lucent stole the thunder with a bid price of 14 billion RMB. Alcatel-Lucent was founded in Paris on 2 December 2006 by Alcatel of France and Lucent of the USA. Its equipment was advanced and competitive. This industry big shot bid a price that no domestic company would dare to match. Clearly, they didn't take Huawei and ZTE seriously.

Other companies started to bid. Two ZTE managers bid 7 billion RMB, half of the Alcatel-Lucent price. ZTE was determined to win this order.

What shocked the five opponents in the bid was that Huawei, who was not taken seriously in CDMA construction, offered a breathtaking price – 690 million RMB, which was a tenth of ZTE's bid and a twentieth of Alcatel-Lucent's. Was this their rock bottom price, or was it suicide?

Brand professionals from ZTE later said: "This happened a lot in bidding events in the telecom industry ... Since Huawei was too aggressive, ZTE had to lower their anticipation by 40%, and cut down the bid price."

The lower bid price by Huawei was a door-in-the-face technique, to get into the CDMA network, and seize more market share in the later upgrading. Even though Huawei didn't make a profit in CDMA construction, it would be compensated for in network maintenance and upgrading. According to industry professionals, the CDMA network of China Telecom would be upgraded to CDMA2000.

Though this construction order was as big as 15 billion RMB, the fees for upgrading and maintenance could be ten times higher.

Ren Zhengfei said: "Each department in Huawei needs to have integrated a 'wolf and bei' plan; aggressive, as well as calculating."

After a fierce battle, the CDMA network bidding settled. Huawei got the orders for major cities like Beijing, Guangzhou, Xi'an and Urumchi, accounting for 25%-26% of the total, ZTE 22%-23%, Alcatel-Lucent 17% ranking third, and Motorola fourth.

The essence of wolf culture was aggressiveness; of bei culture, strategy. Brawn with no brain was reckless; brain with no brawn was cowardly. The combination of aggressiveness and strategy was the essential means for Huawei to conquer the field and expand the market.

In early March 2001, the fifth biggest telecom operator, China Railcom of China, was founded. The project of national switch network remodelling with an investment of 7.2 billion RMB was the first phase of its foundation network construction. The bid for equipment suppliers was worth 820 million RMB. China Railcom planned to attract 15 million users within the first three years it made its debut in the telecom market through high quality network services. The project of local network construction was also known as the "China Railcom First Project", and the headquarters selected three prominent bidders: Huawei, ZTE and the integrated corporation of Shanghai Bell and Beijing Bell.

Ren Zhengfei valued this First Project very much, and instructed the sales department: "This is not a simple sales project. It has a direct impact on the future market structure strategically. Take it as a battle!"

Huawei didn't get any advantages in China Railcom's project, since it had used only a small share of Huawei's equipment. The relationship between the two companies was not close. In contrast, it used over 8,000 Bell brand switch units and the Ministry of Railways held Bell's share. With this connection, Bell had more advantages in terms of customer relations.

Huawei adjusted the strategy according to the circumstances and decided to win the trust of the clients of China Railcom first. When the clients worked in network design, sales associates from Huawei worked together with them till midnight for a few years. They exceeded clients' expectations in many ways and built connections with them.

After the relationship was built, Huawei staff came to promote products in subtle ways, and won the approval of the clients of China Railcom. As well as the additional functions of billing, the Huawei switches could save a fortune for China Railcom. For the first project phase, 37,000 switch units were provided, all by Huawei.

The failure of Bell and ZTE in the first phase of the China Railcom First Project provoked intense promotion in the second phase. To win this battle, sales staff from Huawei developed a few important clients at China Railcom through connections, who brought the switch orders to over 300,000 units. The demands from China Railcom provided bigger markets and profit margins for Huawei.

As the bid for the second phase project approached, the competition of the three providers ramped up. Bell and ZTE continued to come out with favourable terms to take the market. Meanwhile, higher officials at China Railcom were inclined to Bell because of previous cooperation.

Huawei offered favourable terms: if customers bought over 240,000 switches from Huawei, it would give another 8,000 for free.

The huge concessions proved Huawei's seriousness about the deal. In the bid for the second phase, customers weathered the pressure from higher levels and ordered almost 290,000 switches worth 100 million RMB from Huawei. So far, Huawei's switches dominated the China Railcom network. In this sales combat, Huawei didn't send out gifts or engage in any malpractice. It won by sincere offers, and China Railcom customers got high value services. Huawei's triumph was a perfect combination of the wolf and bei culture.

Wolf culture played a crucial part in the startup of the company, driving it snowballing from a little-known small company. If Huawei was the wolf in the beginning, those multinational telecom giants were a group of lions. The wolf's tactics of sudden attack, long-range raids and teamwork encroached on the territory of lions, and made for a lethal attack when the lions were worn out.

Ren Zhengfei led a group of wolves to drive Huawei into the Fortune 500 list in only 22 years. Such achievement won deep respect for wolf culture.

After 2005, Ren Zhengfei talked less of wolf culture, with a new mission statement in lieu. However, wolf culture was imprinted in each Huawei employee's mind as the most significant part of Huawei culture.

CHAPTER

EXPANDING MARKET

Perseverance wears away the stone.
– Xuzi

When Huawei became the biggest telecom supplier in the domestic market, Ren Zhengfei proposed more challenging tasks. Rather than fix the gaze on the domestic market, Huawei should use its high-quality, cheap-priced products as weapons to 'attack' the base of the giant telecom powers.

To forge iron, the body must itself be strong. To achieve its goals in the global market, Huawei firstly strengthened itself. Ren Zhengfei hired professors from Renmin University of China to counsel Huawei on its mission statement for international expansion. However, Ren Zhengfei experienced two of the biggest crises in his business life during this journey: a lawsuit with Cisco and the harbour incident.

Huawei was in danger. Could Ren Zhengfei pull through these two crises?

BELL, BESIEGED AND ANNIHILATED

*If an invasion is repelled, Why shed
more blood unless compelled?*
– Song of the Frontier by Du Fu

In the late 1980s and early 1990s, the market for program-controlled switches was dominated by multinational companies from seven countries and the Chinese market slowly started to add to this as the eighth. Since different systems were not compatible, customers frequently had problems of unclear calls or dropped lines. This was until the early 1990s when the Chinese government issued a single standard that adopted the No.7 Signalling System for the voice network, and the Intelligent Network Application Protocol (INAP) standard for the intelligent network. The chaos in the Chinese telecom industry halted.

In order to change the adverse situation, the Chinese telecom authority founded a joint venture company, Shanghai Bell, in cooperation with the Bell Company of Belgium.

At the same time, Ren Zhengfei started Huawei; the Chinese telecom market was burgeoning, and many local companies emerged at that time, among which the four most representative telecom suppliers were: Dragon Communication, Datang Telecom, ZET Corporation and Huawei Technologies. The founders were respectively, Wu Jiangxing for Dragon Communication, Zhou Huan for Datang Telecom, Hou Weigui for ZET and Ren Zhengfei for Huawei. The minister of Information Industry made an acronym of the Chinese names of the four companies: "Ju Da Zhong Hua", which meant 'big China'.

As the telecom operators started the large-scale network construction, the telecom infrastructure was developed. The four companies took their stride with telecom reforms and developed rapidly, rooting down in the market.

Both ZET and Huawei were headquartered in Shenzhen. Aware of opportunities in rural markets, they both developed user switches, launched into rural markets, and made their first fortune. They competed with foreign brands in price, in service and in product quality. After a series of battles, the giant multinational companies, who used to dominate the market, dropped off and closed business since the profit was too small even to cover staff salaries.

Only Shanghai Bell remained as a big foreign investment company.

The sales revenue of Bell was 430,000 lines in 1990, but their manufacturing capacity was only 300,000 a year. By 1991, the orders mounted to 700,000 lines; by 1992, 1,260,000 lines; by 1993, 2,700,000 lines, which could occupy even three shifts of staff working non-stop. That was why many telecom bureaus were compelled to choose Huawei: because orders for Bell switches were lining up till the next year.

Shanghai Bell Company swept the domestic market with its S1240 digital switch model, which Huawei's C&C08 couldn't match in stability, quality or outer design.

At first, Huawei's technology was not mature, but its engineers would fly to work on the site to fix the machines day and night once any problems occurred. Good customer relations offset product flaws.

When Huawei was struggling with research on the C&C08 switch with 10,000 lines, Bell had already taken hold of the lead position among telecom suppliers in the domestic market. Even so, the C&C08 had been evaluated to, "have reached an advanced international standard."

Ren Zhengfei realized a slim winning opportunity at close quarters, and made a plan to avoid the enemy's strongholds while striking its weak points in the less developed areas of the northeast, northwest and southwest.

With this strategy, Huawei's sales force laid siege to city after city, and convinced one telecom operator after another. With such effort, Huawei gained a firm foothold in places in the northeast, northwest and southwest areas where the telecom infrastructure was underdeveloped, and established for itself a base market.

Huawei also squeezed the profit margins in these places, completely driving Bell away from the underdeveloped market. Meanwhile, the brutal price war impacted Bell's profits on digital switches in cities too.

To defeat your opponent, you need to keep abreast of their progress at first. To exceed Bell's influence, Huawei obscured itself and nursed vengeance for a few years until 1998, when the sales revenue of Huawei reached 7.18 billion USD, ranking 10th in National Top 100 Electronic Enterprises, and surpassing Bell for the first time. Ren Zhengfei saw the coming opportunity and initiated the exploding battle against Bell in R&D, as well as sales and promotion.

In 1990, Bell accounted for 90% of market shares in the Sichuan province when Huawei entered the market. Huawei's sales staff was fully aware of the fact that none of the local telecom operators would immediately switch to Huawei products, no matter how hard they lobbied.

This preconception was not impossible to break though. Huawei's sales staff shunned product promotion and provided free network access to customers strategically. In the lure of free access, Huawei's network expanded to each corner of Sichuan. New network users were won over, connecting each corner into a web.

With this big web of network access users, Huawei's sales staff took the opportunity to introduce the digital switch. The big sales revenue ensued, and Huawei's switch became a mainstream product in the market on par with Bell's. Now, Huawei accounted for 70% of the new market in Sichuan.

The survival of the fittest is the law of business; no one could change that. When the age of broadband local networks dawned, Huawei became the first choice for customers in this field due its efforts in technological development and marketing. Bell couldn't counter-attack Huawei's market.

In 2002, Alcatel acquired a 51% stock-share of Bell, and founded the Shanghai Bell-Alcatel Company. The fierce competition in the Chinese market and the downturn in the global situation compelled the merging of Alcatel and Lucent in 2006, all business channeling into the new Alcatel-Lucent company. In 2009, by a shareholder vote, the Shanghai Bell-Alcatel Company officially changed its name to the Shanghai Bell Company.

Both Huawei and Bell were looking for survival and development. Their overlapping products led to brutal competition. Huawei won this battle eventually. However, before Ren Zhengfei could savour the joy of victory, an imperative internal reform unfolded before him.

RIVALRY, GROWING TOGETHER IN COMPETITION

We take strong rivals as best teachers. Standing
on the shoulder of giants, our steps will never rest,
and our company will develop in the long haul.
– Ding Liang

ZTE was an old rival of Huawei. ZTE was founded in 1985
in Shenzhen, three years earlier than Huawei. The founder,
Hou Weigui, was originally the technical section chief at the
Shaanxi 691 Aerospace System Plant. He came to Shenzhen
at the age of 42 and started a manufacturing business of
electronic watches and electronic keyboards from scratch.
With his tenacity and hard work, Hou Weigui developed a
small factory registered with 3 million RMB to a telecom
behemoth with tens of billions in revenue each year.

Ren Zhengfei, impatient and resolute due to his military
background, advocated a wolf culture in the early stages of

Huawei's development; Hou Weigui, on the contrary, was gentle and tolerant, low key and prudent, sensitive to market and technology and persistent in that pursuit.

Both fought for survival. They were both located in Shenzhen, and sat down together at the early stages to discuss issues pertaining to the rise of the national telecom industry.

Ren Zhengfei and Hou Weigui both made their first fortune in switch development and sales, and entered into the industry of connecting equipment, mobile communication, and optical fibre transmissions in 1996 to diversify their development. They overlapped in 70% of their offered products. The fierce business war was unveiled this year.

In 1996, Huawei's sales revenue hit 2.6 billion RMB, while ZTE lingered at 680 million RMB. Ren Zhengfei sized up the situation and initiated an attack for a better chance of winning. He organized an elite sales troop, brimming with aggressive wolf culture, who swept the nation.

Swords flashing, blood shed, in battles infused with gun smoke, Huawei and ZTE both had wins and losses.

The competition of these leading telecom companies was under the table at first, but was soon brought onto the stage.

In 1998, in competition for the Huanan and Henan markets, the publicity department of Huawei drew up a product instruction manual favourable to Huawei and detrimental to ZTE. This manual made detailed comparisons of Huawei products with their ZTE counterparts, and suggested the Huawei products performed much better than those of ZTE. This allusive version of instruction manuals was sent to selected potential customers by Huawei staff.

When executives from ZTE learned of this news, they decided to give Huawei a dose of its own medicine. They called a staff meeting deep in the night, and created a similar instruction manual that compared ZTE batteries with Huawei batteries; this caused Huawei a loss in bidding.

Huawei would not give up the battle. Ren Zengfei asked Huawei's lawyers to take the battery instruction manual, which indicated the better performance of ZTE batteries, to the court of Henan and Changsha, and make a lawsuit against ZTE.

A test on Huawei batteries was conducted in a rush, and many errors occurred in some key factors in the ZTE instructions. Huawei's lawyers found that ZTE violated Huawei's legitimate rights due to inaccurate data and technology indicators and demanded a compensation of 12 million yuan and 6 million yuan, respectively.

ZTE hired lawyers and conducted a civil action suit in Zhengzhou and Changsha court on 27 July 1998 and 19 August 1998. The lawyers made the case for Huawei's instruction manual, spread by the Huawei Zhengzhou office and Changsha office that indicated Huawei's product was better than ZTE's.

Huawei's comparison led to misunderstandings of ZTE's products, which violated the Anti-Unfair Competition War, and ZTE demanded a compensation of 15 million and 7.5 million yuan in the courts.

Huawei and ZTE – business competitors at loggerheads – all of a sudden became the plaintiff and the defendant in court. The law was just and merciless. In the four lawsuits, they each won two; Huawei was ordered to pay 1,805,000 yuan to ZTE, and ZTE 890,000 yuan to Huawei in verdict.

A compensation of a million didn't matter to Huawei or ZTE. Also, Huawei's brand became well known in a series of news reports. Huawei was finally accepted by the mainstream market as the national brand flagship, with the philosophy of working for the prosperity of the great motherland, for the revitalization of the Chinese nation, and for the happiness of their own family.

The years from 1995 to 1998 were a crucial period for Huawei to conquer the city market. Ren Zhengfei wanted the whole of major city markets in the three years. As Ren Zhengfei put Huawei banners in cities one after another on a national map, Huawei's sales revenue grew from 8.9 billion to 22 billion yuan between the years 1998 and 2000, while ZTE grew from 4.1 billion to 10.2 billion yuan.

Huawei's sales revenue was twice that of ZTE; Huawei had truly become the 'first telecom supplier' in China.

As Huawei became the first supplier in the domestic telecom market, Ren Zhengfei built up forces to challenge the global telecom giants.

BREAKTHROUGH, WINNERS ARE HEROES

Pitch strong camps; fight till death.
– Zeng Guofan

As Huawei and other national companies waged the price of war in the domestic market, winter dawned on the eight international telecom giants; there was no profit to earn. At the beginning of 2002, NEC and Fujitsu announced they would drop out of the Chinese switch markets respectively.

BTM of Belgium founded a joint venture, the Shanghai Bell Company with Chinese Telecom Department, and engaged in a never-ending competition with Huawei and other national telecom companies. Alcatel merged with Lucent because of market pressure, and reorganized with Shanghai Bell to form one company, for resource integration and effective competition, but the prospect was still not optimistic.

Nortel acquired Bay Networks in 1998. Its leading product was the automatic call distribution system used by paging centres, and its share of that market ranked first in the world. Huawei's technology didn't have an advantage over

Nortel, so it competed in after-sales service with this foreign company. If problems occurred in the equipment acquired by local telecom operators, it at least took Nortel engineers a few days to travel to the spot for maintenance. With its expanded network, Huawei's staff could respond immediately to customer needs and arrive at the spot promptly.

Nortel lost ground, one after another. Even the new president, Mike S. Zafirovski, could not stop its retreat. On 14 January 2009, Nortel announced bankruptcy. This telecom giant from the old times bowed out of the Chinese market.

Lucent was even stronger than Nortel. Its affiliated laboratory, Bell Lab, was known far and wide. In 2000, the headquarters of the Bank of China prepared to set up a national call centre, with IBM as the project contractor. IBM had been partners with Lucent for many years, which added to the difficulty for Ren Zhengfei to take this project. Ren Zhengfei sized the situation, and issued instructions to get this contract through PR activities. Huawei sent the best PR staff, impressed the customer after a series of presentations, and won the national call centre contract from the Bank of China headquarters.

In Huawei's aggressive assault, Lucent became overwhelmed. On 3 April 2006, Shanghai Bell Alcatel announced the acquisition of Lucent through the media.

In 1876, Ericsson was founded in Stockholm, the capital of Sweden. It started as a telephone and program-controlled switches producer, and grew to become the world's largest mobile communications equipment manufacturer. In the field of telecoms, Ericsson's product line was relatively simple, the main profit mainly derived from the wireless service as a well-deserved leader in the field of WCDMA. It didn't invest much in switchboard research and development. In the cutthroat switchboard market, Ericsson's leader clearly realized that the cost of human resources and operations rendered them noncompetitive to Huawei or other Chinese companies. Ericsson soon disbanded the switch R&D team and gave up this market, and no longer competed with Huawei in this area.

The defeat of Ericsson was another periodical triumph for Huawei. What Ren Zhengfei didn't expect was a big internal threat as Huawei expanded.

CHANGE, AS SUDDEN AS A STORM

What's coming will come.
You can't escape.
– Internet slogan

The fuse of this threat was Li Yinan.

At the end of 2000, Li Yinan, with an equity settlement and dividends, and equipment worth 10 million yuan, went to Beijing and founded the Beijing Harbor Network Limited. Harbor Network was the premier distributor of Huawei corporate products. After six monthes, Li Yinan was not satisfied with being just a Huawei distributor and launched his own line of products. Harbor Network aimed to "build broadband IP networks for a new economy", and focused on the development of IP network infrastructure, encompassing product development, marketing and sales, technical support and after-sales service, to provide new broadband IP network solutions to telecom operators, enterprises, government agencies and service providers.

With a reputation established at Huawei, Li Yinan was

well known in the telecom industry. Venture capitalists acted immediately to approach Li Yinan at Harbor Network.

All venture capitalists repeated the same fact: It was not necessary for them to invest if Harbor Network could only gain slight profits by distributing Huawei's products. If Li Yinan could develop his own products and go public, they would invest a lot more in him.

Harbor Network was a small, new business and couldn't afford to train new employees for a year as Huawei did. Li Yinan didn't have the time for that. All he could do was to use his influence inside Huawei to poach his old colleagues, the elite research and sales staff from Huawei.

To boost the confidence of his investors, Li Yinan launched self-developed routers, switches and other products within a year of his company's establishment. Harbor Network then entered the broadband IP market, and acquired a market share as high as 7% to 8%, due to its new technology and marketing efforts.

After many years of struggles, Huawei's market share in the broadband IP field was only about 10% to 15%. Li Yinan copied Ren Zhengfei's strategies of business and personnel management, and Harbor Network was dubbed as 'Little Huawei' in the industry.

Li Yinan kept a low profile on purpose and never mentioned Huawei again. However, a high degree of overlapping products led to unavoidable competition between the two companies. With two venture capital investments and his personal intelligence, Li Yinan developed Harbor Network telecom's equipment quickly, which was superior to Huawei's products in technology and function. Huawei's monopoly on the domestic telecom market was threatened by the 'dark horse' – Harbor Network.

In 2003, Huawei's domestic sales revenue hit 15 billion, and Harbor Network one twelfth of this.

Li Yinan was smart. Harbor Network's was like a steamboat compared to the aircraft carrier that was Huawei. The reason he had the courage to initiate the competition and seize Huawei's market was the confidence in his technology, and the lawsuit Huawei was embroiled in with Cisco for infringing on their products.

Caught by the attack of Harbor's intrusion on the market and Cisco's lawsuit, Huawei was in the biggest crisis since its establishment.

LAWSUIT, AN INTERNATIONAL LITIGATION

Let it break in all its fury!
– Song of the Stormy Petrel by Maxim Gorky

Cisco Systems was a world leader among internet solutions providers headquartered in San José, California. It developed software and equipment for internet access. In 1993, Cisco built the world's first internet connected by 1000 routers, and entered the high-speed internet development age. John Chambers joined Cisco in 1991 and became its president in 1996.

Huawei used to focus on voice and traffic equipment. As the market saturated in 1991, Huawei entered the data business for the first time. As it launched routers, ethernets and other major data businesses, it started to branch out in the domestic market with competitive products. Huawei's market share in the data service sector was running neck and neck with Cisco.

In June 2002, Huawei sent their elite marketing staff to promote the company's best products in a telecom equipment exhibition held in Atlanta, US. Shortly after the exhibition started, a gentleman with a big nose and a pair of keen eyes showed up in Huawei's booth. He enquired into details about the major products of telecom equipment and data service of different levels. Huawei's manager at the exhibition took him as a potential customer and answered each of his enquires. After the middle-aged man left, with a serious expression on his face, it dawned on the manager that this middle-aged man was one of the world's best businessmen, John Chambers.

After Chambers returned to his company, he immediately set up a special group to combat Huawei. A plan was drafted in quick action. After Chambers approved, it came into practice.

In June of the same year, Huawei found its American company, Future Wei, in Santa Clara, California. In order to rally the new company, they designed posters of their latest products with the Golden Gate Bridge in the background, and a slogan that read: "The only difference is price."

Cisco and other American local brands could never sit still under the pressure of falling market shares and the waves of Huawei's sales campaign. In January 2003, Cisco hired a group of US attorneys specializing in intellectual property to form a strong litigation team, and filed a complaint over 70 pages long in the Marshall Federal Court in Texas, United States. In Cisco's complaint, Huawei was sued for four aspects: copying Cisco's IOS source code, using Cisco's technical documents, duplicating command line interface, and violating at least of five of Cisco's patents.

In response, Huawei quickly set up a team composed of elite staff from departments of intellectual property, law, data products, research and development, and marketing.

This team was led by Guo Ping, Xu Wenwei, Feimin, Hong Tianfeng and a few other Huawei vice presidents, and they flew to America for the case.

HANDSHAKING, TO FORGO OLD GRUDGES IN SMILE

The world is the sea, drowning those who can't swim.
– Spanish proverb

At the beginning of the lawsuit, Huawei was in the wrong, according to public opinion. Lawyers hired by Cisco were experts in technology patent lawsuits. Issues with vague boundaries, after processing and over analyzing, became the evidence of Huawei's infringement on Cisco's intellectual properties.

Huawei always kept low key, but Cisco had already devoted itself to a 150 million USD advertising campaign before this lawsuit. US media only knew Cisco, not Huawei. They didn't know there was a Chinese company across the ocean that could manufacture such advanced telecom and internet products. Thus, at the beginning of this international lawsuit, American media unanimously reported that Huawei had 'stolen' Cisco's patent.

A more severe situation was taking place in the home-land. Except for a few neutral media sources, many reputable Chinese media reported clearly on Cisco's side. Though the biggest telecom and internet manufacturer, Huawei was not well known; government and media alike didn't know of it at all. It didn't have much communication or connection with the government, and didn't receive any of the government's support in this.

Guo Ping was deeply aware of the power of public communication. He wrote an article dozens of pages long in counteraccusation, in which he explained, in professional and scientific terms, that Huawei didn't infringe on Cisco's patent. This international lawsuit aimed to stop Huawei in American markets, and avoid the competition legally.

Guo Ping approached Edelman Public Relations Worldwide, and met with American media through it. In the subsequent press conference, he communicated with reporters from Fortune, *The Wall Street Journal* and other press, to explain the real Huawei. Then, they invited lawyers to visit Huawei's R&D centre in China, to get them to understand Huawei's technology capacity and dispel the influence of Cisco's propaganda.

Early in 2003, Huawei and Cisco had their first trial in the Marshall Federal Court. Huawei spent a fortune to hire the famous American lawyer, Robert Haslam, a top attorney in the field of intellectual property litigation, who was the lawyer of Microsoft in their antitrust case. He was proficient in law and had rich experience in intellectual property cases.

Robert Haslam studied Cisco's indictment back and forth, and decided on a strategy of counteracting with Guo Ping. The plan was to make an issue on Cisco's 'proprietary protocol', which was owned by a single organization in the market before international standards and norms of the communication and networking formed. Once proprietary protocol became the de facto, the enterprise of the ownership could grow to a monopoly in the market. In the court and in the media, Huawei was focused on Cisco's attempt to monopolize the market and prelude business competition.

As well as for the trial, Guo Ping had come to the USA with a secret mission, which was to negotiate business cooperation with the 3Com Corporation. On 20 March 2003, Huawei and 3Com found a joint venture, which would be engaged in the research, development and sales of data telecom products in America.

Before the second trial, Ren Zhengfei asked Guo Ping to invite a third-party expert, a data communications professor from Stanford, to Huawei headquarters, and invited him to compare and analyze Cisco's IOS platform and Huawei's VRP platform. The analysis showed Cisco's IOS platform had 20 million lines of source code while Huawei's VRP platform had only 2 million lines, of which only 1.9% overlapped with Cisco's proprietary protocol. The conclusion from the third-party expert was simple: with only 2 million lines of source code, how could Huawei's software plagiarize Cisco's which was 10 times bigger?

On 26 March 2003, in the second trial, Huawei's lawyers defended the case by counterclaiming Cisco's compensation for its negative influence on Huawei's performance in the American market.

The CEO of 3Com, Claflin, testified before the court: Huawei was accountable for its technological capacity. He also told the American media: "Huawei has numerous talented engineers, who operate the most advanced equipment and software in their large offices. Huawei owns the most advanced robot equipment I have ever seen."

The testimonies of Claflin led Americans to re-examine Huawei, this Chinese telecom network company. They trusted the testimonies of the 3Com Corporation since it was a US company.

After a series of efforts, the dynamic in the court changed from a lawsuit of a Chinese company for intellectual property infringement, to an antitrust, anti-oppression case fought by two small companies, Huawei and 3Com, together.

Cisco's lawyers played their trump card, to request the court to examine the source code of the software of both companies, since it was crucial to identify property infringement. Cisco's lawyer, Mark Chandler, was confident: "We look forward to examining the source code of Huawei's software."

On 1 October 2003, lawyers from both sides finished the comparison of the source codes, and proved the legitimacy of Huawei's source code. The American court, in an attempt to quieten down the matter and give an out for the national business, issued its judgment: to order Huawei to stop using some source code, the operation interface and online help documents as proposed controversial by Cisco.

On 2 October 2003, Cisco and Huawei reached a preliminary settlement agreement. By the end of July 2004, they reached a final settlement agreement. This one-year lawsuit finally settled. Cisco won face, and Huawei won substance. The lawsuit not only didn't stop Huawei's steps to enter the American market, but provided free publicity of Huawei products to the world. By overwhelming media coverage, Americans got the message: "Huawei is coming! Huawei is coming!"

COMBAT, ACQUIRING HARBOR NETWORK

**Mishaps are like knives, that either serve us or
cut us, as we grasp them by the blade or the handle.
– James Lowell**

As Huawei finished the lawsuit with Cisco in 2003, Ren Zhengfei finally had the time and energy to fight back aginst Li Yinan in the domestic market. In 2002, Ren Zhengfei ordered to retract Huawei's dealership with Harbor Network.

A special office to combat Harbor Network was set up, with the single objective of attacking Harbor Network and stopping its threat to Huawei. Ren Zhengfei laid a few ground rules for this special office from the beginning: 1) It didn't matter if Huawei lost contracts because of ZTE or Cisco, but sales staff would be severely punished or even dismissed if they lost them because of Harbor Network; 2)

Huawei would give free data access and projects to big Harbor Network clients. If they were using Harbor Network products, Huawei would purchase them, and give a 'two for one' discount to them for Huawei products, which aimed to block Harbor Network's business; 3) To poach back talented people who worked for Harbor Network at any cost.

To mobilize this special office, Ren Zhengfei created the "combat Harbor Network" fund, which reached 40 million yuan within one year.

To command this special office, Huawei gave play to the wolf culture and expanded the market in all directions. The market share of Harbor Network waxed and waned. After the glory of 2003, Li Yinan found the market was harsh in 2004, and he couldn't collect payments on the goods that were sold.

The effect of poaching back talent was obvious too. Many R&D staff working in the network connection at Harbor network quit and joined Huawei.

As the operation declined, venture capitalists became uninvolved and stopped investing in Li Yinan. After deliberation, Li Yinan regarded going public as the only way to come back to life.

Li Yinan needed a breakthrough for Harbor Network, but Ren Zhengfei had already instructed the special office to stop Harbor Network going public.

According to the Securities Law of the People's Republic of China, the enterprise who applied to go public needed a three years' record of non-violation of law.

Harbor Network started the listing process in the US NASDAQ twice. Each time the US Securities & Switch Commission received a large number of anonymous letters to sue Harbor Network for infringement or other issues.

The investigation of these issues needed a few years. A Harbor Network manager in charge of the listing process lamented: "Upon receipt of such letters, the whole process would be dragged down. In many cases, you could do nothing but give up."

The company couldn't go public. The last resort for Li Yinan was to sell the company, since all ways to break through Huawei's attack were blocked.

At the end of 2005, Warburg Pincus Investment finally found a big buyer for Li Yinan – Siemens. Siemens was a strong rival of Huawei, both at home and abroad. Ren Zhengfei would not allow its acquisition of Harbor Network. In order to stop the acquisition, the 'poaching team' bent backwards to poach the voice research group of Harbor Network Research Institute in Shenzhen at the cost of 10 million yuan.

Harbor Network's VOLP business couldn't survive without the support of the voice research group. After this group was gone, VOLP business was immediately wiped out. Harbor Network was no longer attractive for Siemens. Ren Zhengfei set up another insurmountable threshold of intellectual property rights for Siemens' acquisition. Siemens also worried about potential lawsuits after the acquisition and halted signing the contract. The plan to sell to Siemens died halfway. With pressure from shareholders, Li Yinan only had one way to go, that is, to sell Harbor Network to Huawei.

On 10 May 2006, Ren Zhengfei and Li Yinan met at Huawei 3Com headquarters in Hangzhou. Ren Zhengfei took Li Yinan's hand and said: "Your return was a contribution to the history of the development of Chinese technology. It's not that you lost – we win. We both win."

The acquisition of Harbor Network manifested Huawei's dominating position in the domestic telecom industry. It also deliberately warned any latecomers who wanted to fight against Huawei that its dominance could not be coveted or challenged.

CHAPTER

6

WORLD
IN HAND

Great ambition brings distant land closer.
– Cao Zhi

On 11 December 2001, China officially joined the World
Trade Organization as its 143rd member. After joining
the WTO, all Chinese enterprises were confronted with
battles in the journey of globalization and going out for
further development.

HONG KONG, ENACTING NUMBER PORTABILITY

Courage leads to heaven; fear leads to death.
– Seneca

The international market was truly a big one. In the report 'Current Situation and Our Mission', Ren Zhengfei wrote: "Without independent national industry, there would be no national independence. Our main task for the next five years is to be in line with international practice, in R&D systems, in manufacturing equipment and management, and in corporate culture and management."

Opportunities favour those who are prepared. In 1996, a Hong Kong telecom company, Hutchison Telecom, a subsidiary to the richest Chinese, Li Ka-shing, approached Huawei for it had just received a license for landline phone services, and needed to enact number portability within three months. Hutchison Telecom took the matter seriously and flew to every possible equipment provider in Europe, but got the exact same answer that the project needed at least six months to complete, at a very expensive price.

As they were agitated like ants in a hot pan, someone from the industry recommended Huawei to them.

Huawei's price and schedule met their exact requirements. They immediately signed the contract after discussion. However, as Huawei's C&C08 switch was transported to Hong Kong, problems occurred even before adjustment. As an inch of land is worth gold in Hong Kong, the operating room in Hong Kong was much smaller than that of the office in mainland China and could not fit Huawei's switch cabinet.

With this feedback from Hong Kong, Ren Zhengfei made the immediate instruction that: "Hong Kong is the first stop to overtaking the overseas markets. We must overcome all difficulties."

Huawei R&D staff responded immediately, and quickly developed a wall-mounted remote terminal, specifically for Hong Kong. To ensure number portability, Huawei installed a customized NP function. As with the installation of the C&C08 wall-mounted switch in Hong Kong, the problem of incompatibility with original Hutchison switches arose.

The installation engineers realized the weight on their shoulders. They gave up weekends and holidays, lived in the cramped operating room, tested and adjusted time and time again, until the incompatibility issue was finally solved.

In less than three months, Huawei completed this project. The advantage in price and newly added functions made Hutchison's customers unable to put it down. The wall-mounted Huawei equipment could even fit under a staircase, accommodating to the compact city environment of Hong Kong.

After adaption, Huawei's C&C08 wall-mounted switch maintained stable and smooth connections for landlines. It passed inspections and received an operation license in Hong Kong. Other Huawei products quickly spread soon after that. In a short time, over twenty telecom bureaus switched to Huawei products, and Huawei's business covered major business districts, over 3,000 office buildings, and the airport in Hong Kong, a reliable resource for telecoms in the 'dynamic capital of Asia'.

AFRICA, I AM COMING FOR VICTORY

**If a man carries a jar of water over
his head, his brothers won't thirst.
– African proverb**

Africa literally means 'piercing sunlight'. International tele-com giants mostly focused on the affluent markets in Europe and America. Their investment in Africa was limited to a few big cities. When Huawei's staff arrived in Africa, they found that western telecom companies monopolized the fundamental telecom market; the price in the region was ridiculously high, and the service was inefficient. This unhealthy market structure made it possible for Huawei to enter this market.

Huawei's sales staff came to Mauritius in mid-summer. The moment they got off the plane, they were blinded by the dazzling sunlight; surging waves of heat engulfed them, rushing them to a dizzy and blurry world. Their clothing could be wrung out, yielding a stream of sweat.

The average age of staff overseas was 27. This group of young people, in an unfamiliar environment, needed to survive first, and then go on a quest for customers.

The competitive advantage of Huawei products in terms of price and sales service won sales staff the first WCDMD business contract in Mauritius. Huawei, from China, became the contractor that would build its 3G network.

Nigeria, the most populated country in Africa, was plagued by conflict between various ethnic groups and complicated regional branches. Lead by Wang Junqiang, Huawei's sales staff flew to this country comprised of 250 ethnic groups, and started to work in the unstable environment.

The landline phone market was monopolized by Siemens and Alcatel; Ericsson dominated the mobile market. Telecom operators there only recognized the big global brands and were indifferent to Huawei's products.

Wang Junqiang led the sales staff to fight for a year with little achievement. Since the market in big cities was not open in Nigeria, Wang Junqiang decided to transfer to remote areas to promote sales.

After some endeavour, they finally sold a 1000-line switch module worth 2 million USD in a remote town, but the Nigerian clients requested TK construction services from Huawei engineers, a customized telecom network construction project including site selection, operation room design, outer pipeline design, etc.

Sales associates in Huawei had never provided TK construction services to telecom operators. The profit earned by a 2 million USD piece of equipment was too low to cover these services. It was promotion over profit. Wang Junqiang thought back and forth, and decided do it at their own cost.

Huawei's first project in Nigeria didn't make any profit, but it trained the team, familiarizing them with the clients' concerns and requirements, different from those of home.

After Huawei gained a foothold in Nigeria, they invested 20 million USD, without flinching, to build the only telecom operator training centre in West Africa to introduce more technicians into the telecom sphere through training and the transfer of technology.

With unremitting efforts, Huawei finally signed a GSM base transceiver station supply contract worth 80 million USD with the second biggest Nigerian telecom operator, Vmobile, and contracted the construction of the longest transmission network in the Southern part of Africa, covering all major cities in Nigeria.

Whereas Huawei's accomplishment in Nigeria was difficult, their endeavours in the Democratic Republic of the Congo were precarious. On 8 April 2005, Liu Kang came alone as a pioneer to the Democratic Republic of the Congo for business opportunities. In account of difficult entrepreneurship, he said: "The infrastructure in the Democratic Republic of the Congo was weak; there were no roads in many places, rather the installation of base transceiver stations and their adjustment were always located in a field. It was common for Huawei engineers to drive for three to four days to work at a field site, where no traces of human life could be found. We always brought a few bottles of water and some bread for food. We slept in the car and ate only bread most of the time. If there was hot water for instant noodles with Lan Ganma chilli paste, it was a feast for us."

You could grit your teeth and push through the harsh environment, prepare and protect yourself from the rampant malaria, but you couldn't have predicted the intense gunshots, followed by heavy artillery, after the election on 20 July, 2006, at 18:30.

In the most intense fights, apartment buildings where Huawei staff lived were besieged by opposing armed forces, the sort of scene you expect from a Hollywood movie: bullets were flying, bombs exploded, blood converged to streams, and dead bodies were scattered everywhere. Fortunately, this conflict ended soon, and the Democratic Republic of the Congo resumed to normality.

In 2006, Huawei earned a contract worth 100 million USD from mobile operator Oasis Sprl in order to construct a GSM network for them.

Huawei's EnerGGSM solution could effectively reduce the construction and maintenance costs and improve network efficiency. The new generation of DD base transceiver stations had features like high integration and strong receiving sensitivity; they were welcomed by global GSM operators right after launch.

After experiencing the stable, efficient and advanced qualities of Huawei products, the CEO of Oasis Sprl said: "The cooperation with Huawei was a milestone for both sides, which pushed Oasis Sprl into new telecom fields. The partnership with Huawei made us more competitive in the mobile market and improved customer satisfaction."

Huawei made remarkable achievements in Nigeria and the Democratic Republic of the Congo, as well as in Kenya and Algeria. Huawei's sales revenue in South Africa reached a billion USD, as its products spread over South Africa.

INDIA: DISPLAYING CAPABILITY IN DIFFICULTY

To catch a black sheep in the daylight.
– Anon proverb

The third issue of the Roland Bell Telecom Review of 2005 had descriptions of the Indian telecom market: India, the last non-fully developed telecom market, was developing with a 50% growth rate; there were 50 million users right now, and this number would exceed 200 million in a few years.

With his keen business vision, Ren Zhengfei couldn't miss the excellent opportunities in the Indian market. Huawei entered India pretty early.

In Indian Essays, Ren Zhengfei wrote: "Many doctoral research projects, like broadband, algorithms of high-frequency radio waves, were evaluated as excellent world-class projects by experts in the trip. Indian doctoral candidates were poor, dressed in broken slippers and ragged clothes, like our old-school years.

Impoverished as Indian engineers were, they worked hard and made India a big source of software exportation. In June 1999, Huawei opened a research institute in Bangalore, the 'Silicon Valley' of India; however, some Huawei employees who relocated to India thought "the investment outweighed the gains."

In Ren Zhengfei's opinion, there were many CMM certified companies in India. Huawei's research institute was a perfect platform to attract talented local engineers.

In 2001, Huawei officially established a R&D centre in India, and recruited 1,000 employees, which made it Huawei's biggest R&D centre abroad. In 2002, Huawei's products entered the Indian market. As sales revenues escalated, Huawei formed partnerships with Tata Teleservices and others.

Ren Zhengfei's expectations were soon achieved. On 1 August, Huawei's Indian R&D centre was fifth level certified by the CMM.

The CMM is a capacity maturity model developed by SEI Carnegie Mellon University, and defined its five levels as Initial, Repeatable, Defined, Managed, to Optimizing. The software process is believed to improve as the organization moves up each level, with shorter production cycles and lower costs.

The fifth level certification earned by Huawei's Indian R&D centre marked another significant progress Huawei had achieved in telecom and software development, another proof of Huawei's capacity for software development, in line with advanced international standards.

Due to some historical issues and a 'Chinese Threat' theory advocated by western countries, India's telecom regulators imposed strict restrictions on Huawei's business; they even banned local telecom operators from buying equipment from Huawei and other Chinese companies on the grounds that 'espionage' technology may be inserted into their products and jeopardize national security.

Not only did Indian regulation authorities set limitations on Huawei, but they 'ordered' that Chinese telecom companies revealed their ownership details within a month, to prove that there was no military influence in the company.

In order to relieve these concerns, Huawei sent senior vice president Xu Zhijun to meet with the Indian government, who had misread Huawei's operation deeply. They asked Xu Zhijun: "Is it true that only Chinese engineers are allowed to participate in the core projects at Huawei's Indian R&D centre, and Indian engineers are excluded?"

To lift the Indian government's concerns, Xu Zhijun organized tours of Huawei's R&D centre for engineers from local companies. Vice president of the Indian R&D centre, head of development and engineering, Gupta said: "We established this R&D centre before entering the Indian market. Ninety nine per cent of our engineers are Indian; there are only about 30 Chinese employees here to aid in the transfer of technology, technology design and customer interface support. The laboratories and research equipment are equally open to both Chinese and Indian engineers."

The vice president of Huawei Indian Company, Yao Weimin, set up a strict rule for Chinese employees, that is, to wear Indian garb while at work. Yao Weimin also donned Rajeev as his Indian name. To take root in India, they needed to conform to the 'identity', and manage it well.

On 14 May 2010, to completely dispel the concerns of the Indian government, Ren Zhengfei announced that

Huawei was willing to open their source code for others to look at to see if they could detect any threat. Software source code is the most valuable asset for a company, and Huawei had shown it genuinely to the Indian government.

Restrictions in the market made Huawei's annual revenue drop from 2 billion USD in 2009 to 0.8 billion USD in 2013.

The CEO of Huawei Indian Company told a reporter from the Economic Times: "Despite business decline in the past few years, we are keeping our investments. The security issues have passed. Government and operators understand us now."

EUROPE: DOING BUSINESS GRACEFULLY

A nail is driven out by another nail;
habit is overcome by habit.
– Erasmus

Chen Haijun was sent to expand the market in the Netherlands. Surprisingly, he found a business opportunity in a casual conversation with a business manager from Telfort who had received a 3G license in July 2000, but hadn't started the 3G business yet.

Why didn't they start the business? Chen Haijun searched for the reasons and found the salve for the sore. The market in the Netherlands had opened to Huawei.

In 2003, Chen Haijun was sent to the Netherlands for market expansion. As one of the most developed countries in Western Europe, the competition in the mobile business was intense; five mobile operators vied for the market: four giant multinational companies: Vodafone, Orange, T Mobile, KPN; and one local company, Telfort, a fast developing and leading local operator, which was lauded as the best network service by the Independent Customers Organization.

One day in June, Chen Haijun met a business manager from Telfort for the first time via an introduction by a friend in the telecom bureau. They felt like old friends upon their first meeting. During the conversation, Chen Haijun realized that Telfort had received a 3G license in July 2000, but held back from developing the 3G business.

The reason was simple: Telfort, the least established among the five telecom companies, was worried that its research and technology couldn't catch up with 3G network requirements, and they needed to consider the development situation in the Netherlands.

The Netherlands had the densest population in Europe and took environmental protection very seriously. Besides the cost of base transceiver station construction and equipment, they needed to consider the compensation for architecture owners on their approval. All added up: 3G became a piece of fool's gold to Telfort.

Chen Haijun developed the plan for separable base transceiver stations to accommodate Telfort's situation, in which BBU and RRU were two independent parts. The equipment could be installed in original Telfort cabinets or poles and walls close to antennae. This plan was viable and cost-effective, 1/3 less than the common practice.

Telfort accepted Chen Haijun's plan, and Huawei engineers were sent for construction in an orderly manner. The project was completed by the end of the year. As proven through testaments, Telfort was satisfied with the 3G network built by Huawei.

Huawei immediately won the Netherlands' market. Its efficient and cost-effective services were spread by word of mouth among telecom operators. On 7 June, Hauwei signed a contract with KPN as its only equipment supplier for its national backbone transmission network.

On February 2010, French telecom operator NEUF launched a project to build a backbone optical transmission network across France. The objective was that for 30 euros each month, users could enjoy a selection of 160 digital television channels, internet access and telephone services. The 'three-in-one' high value service was a very innovative concept, and an attractive solution to customer needs.

Before launching the project, the CEO of NEUF, Michel Paulin, had already drafted a suppliers list. Huawei was not included.

In order to make it on the suppliers list, Huawei approached a NEUF agent close to them. After the agent inspected Huawei's products, he made a serious call to Michel Paulin, recommending Huawei for the suppliers' competition.

NEUF was a newly founded network operator, and didn't have any experience in cooperating with Chinese companies. After deliberate consideration of the phone call, Michel Paulin made the decision to approve Huawei to participate in the bidding for the optical transmission project.

Huawei was confident in its optical fibre network capacity, and offered a generous deal to NEUF: Huawei was going to build the NEUF optical fibre network in two representative cities and would remain responsible for the operation for three months. By then, NEUF could conduct evaluation and acceptance.

Sure enough, Huawei mobilized its brilliant engineers and completed optical fibre network constructions in two cities within three months, handing off to NEUF a mature and stable network after testing and adaptation.

The price, speed and stability of Huawei's products won over NEUF. They gave thumbs up to Huawei engineers. In the next few years, Huawei got the contract to construct an optical fibre network construction across France from NEUF.

Michel Paulin commented on the cooperation with Huawei: "We achieved the speed we desired. The market was dominated by France Telecom a few years ago, and now we have become its biggest rival. Why? Because we acted fast and took risks, and of course, we are a little cheaper, thanks to our Chinese provider. Huawei saved us at least 10% in investment."

If we can attribute Huawei's success in France to confidence, then in the UK it was to do with capacity.

British Telecom (BT) was a public-sector organization originally run by British Postal Administration. In 1980, it broke away from Royal Mail and became an independent state-owned business. It was the biggest telecom hardware operator in the UK.

In 2005, BT launched a project called the "Network of the 21st Century", a deliberate framework for boosting the whole telecom industry. An investment of 10 billion GBP would be allocated to keep the UK ahead in telecom innovation, and shorten the market cycle.

Huawei's representative in the UK, Cui Junhai, participated in the first bidding for the "Network of the 21st Century" project in June 2005. Since he had taken office, Cui Junhai had spent over a year communicating with BT and modifying the price of offer over five or six rounds, but gained nothing. A conversation with a friend made him realize that multinational corporations like BT would have fixed suppliers on a shortlist to choose the final candidate.

To make it on to BT's shortlist was not simple. Huawei needed to be evaluated on 12 categories by BT's experts to get certified.

Huawei's philosophy was to 'take the bull by the horns' through thick and thin. Ren Zhengfei called a meeting specifically for this, where he and Huawei executives reached a consensus of inviting BT experts to inspect Huawei for certification, and taking it as the test for entering the British market. The preparation committee was founded later with chairwoman Sun Yafang and general vice president Fei Min as leaders, excellent staff from sales, marketing, supply chain management, human resources, and finance as members.

The bold move to invite BT experts for certification was proof of Huawei's excellence. Ren Zhengfei took the model of IBM and brought IPD management in 1998, and ISC systems in 2000. The management, R&D and sales had been upgraded a few levels to be in line with multinational companies like IBM.

In November 2013, BT's Procurement Certification Group went to Huawei and inspected the facilities for four days in the fields of product and solution quality, development strategy, management systems, quality control systems, project management and corporate social responsibility.

In addition to the business operation items listed above, the investigation was based on the credibility of Huawei's business partners, the accuracy of product supplies, and even the level of human dignity indicated by the conditions of canteens and dormitories for employees. In the five main categories, Huawei won four As and one A-.

In the meantime, some management vulnerability was exposed in the examination of world class experts. When someone in the expert groups asked: "From the perspective of whole flow, who can tell me the most important five factors you need to attend to in order to ensure delivering high quality products?"

None of Huawei's experts could answer!

When BT experts inspected the ISC, they posed another question: "How does Huawei ensure timely product delivery?"

Huawei experts answered: "We have a strict assessment system for the product shipment rate."

The BT experts pointed out bluntly: "As customers, we don't care about your shipment rate; we care about your timely delivery."

Solutions always outnumbered problems. Vulnerability evolved to advantage. It took Huawei years and billions of dollars to enter BT's shortlist. Huawei's management lived up to international suppliers' standards through this test.

Huawei successfully entered BT's shortlist. All things come to those who wait. After five years of struggles, Huawei embedded itself in the UK market.

Huawei's products earned a good reputation in the UK market, and Huawei became partners with international tycoons like Vodaphone and BT. In February 2005, Huawei was awarded "Chinese Investor of the Year" by the British Exporters Association; Huawei's efforts had finally been recognized by the UK.

CHAPTER 7

THE EIGHT FACES OF REN ZHENGFEI

**Who am I? Where do I come from?
Where am I going to? – Plato**

From the side, a whole range;
From the end, a single peak;
Far, near, high, low – no two parts alike.
Why can't I tell the true shape of Lu-shan?
Because I myself am in the mountain.
What's the shape of Lushan? No one has the answer. What kind of person is Ren Zhengfei? A thousand answers emerge from a thousand readers.

TEMPER AND AFFABILITY

Man on earth, good at birth.
– Three Character Classic

Ren Zhengfei has a short fuse with high-level management cadres in Huawei, but acts a lenient father or big brother to ordinary employees. He always loses his temper at the things he frowns upon, but he is, on the other hand, flexible.

With his military background, Ren Zhengfei is known to be bad-tempered. His 'direct communication' is a legacy of military culture. Word spread among management executives in Huawei is that it is hard to get Mr Ren's praise, but to be reproached is a daily routine.

Like the majority of military personnel, Ren Zhengfei pursues efficiency, resolution and mental and verbal dexterity. His style of direct communication achieved a high level of efficiency in the conferences he presided over. All speakers cut right to the point. If some irrelevant 'nonsense' popped out occasionally, Ren Zhengfei would either interrupt the speaker, or yell, "Don't fart."

Ren Zhengfei reprimands people harshly, but mostly to management level executives. In the eyes of Huawei's ordinary employees, Ren Zhengfei is a magnanimous gentleman. As Huawei expanded and grew its overseas telecom business, many employees were sent to work abroad. Ren Zhengfei once brought the executive in charge of overseas business management in and told him: "Life is dull for our employees overseas. Send them some good books and DVDs."

In the winter of 2005, a Huawei employee came back to Shenzhen from a business trip and met Ren Zhengfei at the airport. He intended to pretend to not have seen him, but Ren Zhengfei came forward to greet him and asked about his situation. Ren Zhengfei gave a ride to him first before driving back to his own home, which deeply impressed this employee.

GENEROSITY AND PENNY PINCHING

**Keep good company, and you
shall become one of them.
– Encouraging learning**

Money is good. Sometimes you need to be generous and sometimes you need strict budgeting. As the president of Huawei, Ren Zhengfei is a model for employees to follow.

Ren Zhengfei can be very generous, to the degree of astonishing customers. In 2000, Huawei participated in the Hong Kong Telecom Exhibition, and invited over 2000 telecom officials, operators and agents from over 50 countries.

For the 2,000 guests, Huawei provided first or business cabin flight ticket round trips, five star hotels, and a laptop for each of them. The exhibition cost Huawei 200 million HKD. It was the first time that Huawei revealed its power to the international telecom industry. It was proven that Ren Zhengfei's generosity received high returns. Huawei's global expansion started in 2000 with increasing market shares.

Huawei's employees scattered to each corner of the world. Insurance for them was bought from the American AIA Insurance Company, and the annual cost reached 800 billion RMB. If Huawei's employees ran into accidents abroad, helicopters were used to send them to authorized hospitals. It was disclosed by a Huawei employee in Mexico that: "Huawei would rent the best apartments in the nicest neighborhoods for its employees, and provide funding to buy ping pong tables, books and DVDs to enrich their life abroad. Flight tickets for spousal visits were also reimbursed."

Ren Zhengfei rose from poverty. His efforts afforded him any luxurious lifestyle, but he maintained a frugal life. He drove a second-hand Peugeot worth 100,000 RMB until 2000, when he switched to a BMW for safety concerns. He never had a driver. People follow the example of their superiors. Huawei executives didn't drive luxurious cars either.

The style of a president predicts the style of employees. Huawei staff like to eat at the sidewalk snack booths. Even leaders are 'stingy' when they take their staff to eat: a plate of boiled peanuts, a cucumber salad, a bowl of sautéed rice noodles each, in a small restaurant, and twice cooked pork for the sake of savoury.

This was a common menu for a gathering party at Huawei.

RESPONSIBILITY AND LOW PROFILE

A brave heart serves justice.
– Li Dazhao

On 12 May 2008, an earthquake with an 8.0 magnitude struck Wenchuan county, Sichuan and the telecom lines and mobile base transceiver station were destroyed. Wenchuan became an isolated island. No information about the disaster situation or disaster relief could pass in or out.

In an urgent need to recover communication, Ren Zhengfei called for a high executives meeting in Huawei to prepare for disaster relief. Two immediate decisions were made: first, to advocate for donations to the affected area among all Huawei staff; second, to donate a batch of telecom equipment to operators in disaster areas.

Emergency action was taken by Huawei. The company made a 5 million RMB donation, while domestic employees donated 15 million RMB and employees abroad donated 10 million RMB all together. Telecom equipment worth 100 million RMB was also donated. Around 150 of Huawei's technican staff flew from Zhenshen to Chengdu via Chongqing for onsite support, under the leadership of the board chairwoman Sun Yafang, and global sales and service president, Hu Houkun.

Afterwards, 4,000 Huawei 'standby model' mobile phones were airdropped in Wenchuan. This mobile model was developed specifically for harsh environments, as its battery could continue for seven to eight days of normal usage, and it could withstand high pressures and outside impacts – ideal for use in an earthquake.

At 8:15, 16 May, Huawei employee Luo Tao activated the first base transceiver station. At 8:30, the first phone call got through. At the same time, Sichuan Mobile activated five base transceiver stations in the Dujiangyan area with the support of Huawei technicians and equipment.

In the disaster relief for Wenchuan, the equipment and money Huawei donated was the biggest in RMB value among domestic enterprises, but Ren Zhengfei shunned employees from taking interviews. He said: "Donating to the disaster relief was not for show. The time taken by the interview should be used to do some real disaster relief work."

Ren Zhengfei never took interviews from Chinese or international media and has been dubbed as the 'the most mysterious Chinese businessman'. He once said: "In the face of media pressure, the company needs to be an ostrich burying its head in sand."

On 8 May 2013 in New Zealand, Ren Zhengfei announced his retirement plan for the first time and answered questions from a few journalists regarding human rights in China. He satirized the conversation and absurdity of American politicians who attempted to ban Huawei in the name of 'National Safety'. It was his first time to communicating with journalists in 25 years.

Ren Zhengfei met with the French media again on 25 November 2013. A journalist from *Le Monde* asked: "You have been keeping a low profile and keeping distance from the media for all your life. Why did you choose to meet the media this time? Why in France?"

Ren Zhengfei responded: "I am not a low-profile person, otherwise I could not lead tens of tens of thousands of people in Huawei. I would go crazy with the kids at home. My grandchildren in school like to talk to me. I am not such a low-profile person as the media depicts."

Not only did he turn down the position of vice chairman of the all China Federation of Industry and Commerce and deputy to the National People's Congress, but he refused all kinds of different honours. When such a low-profile person claims not to keep a low profile, people laughed.

DICTATORSHIP AND TENDERNESS

**I started to cry since birth, and
repeated my reason each day.
– Jack London**

At the end of November 2007, a total of 7,000 Huawei employees who had each worked for the company for over eight years turned in their resignations. Resigned staff could compete for the same post again, with the same salary and benefits. The only change was that they needed to resign the contract, which would cancel their seniority in the company. Those who resigned and didn't re-contract would receive compensation, the total amount of which reached 1 billion RMB.

This was the incident of the "Ten Thousand People Resignation", which caused a sensation nationwide. To understand the reason for this, you need to understand the work ID number system at Huawei. In Huawei, Ren Zhengfei's work ID number was 001. It followed subsequently for others according to the time they joined Huawei, which was convenient for human resources management, but induced some problems as time went by. Some old employees rested on laurels, and abused their seniority. They didn't work hard, but had good earnings from internal stock shares, which dampened the enthusiasm of new employees, and contradicted the advocated principal of 'dedication' in Huawei. Ren Zhengfei ushered in the Ten Thousand People Resignation, instructing that any employees who worked for Huawei for over eight years needed to resign before the new year of 2008, and re-sign the contract for one to three years after reapplying for their positions.

Those who quit on their own free will would receive due compensation from Huawei. The original work ID number system was suspended and a new work ID system was introduced. Ren Zhengfei set the example himself. After resigning and being rehired for his original position, he would never assign No. 001.

The introduction of the new policy was ridiculed in the media. Many critics believed this was a buy-out offer from Huawei.

Huawei explained to the media that the event of the Ten Thousand People Resignation aimed to end the mindset of 'satisfying with little achievement', to wake up the 'wolf spirit' in Huawei's staff, and boost the competitiveness of the enterprise. With the insistence of Ren Zhengfei, Huawei stood firm against all kinds of pressure, and the event of the Ten Thousand People Resignation finally happened.

Stories about Ren Zhengfei's iron hand seemed to never end, but Huawei's president Ren Zhengfei had another side, that of an ordinary person, a husband, a father, a son – a side of warmth.

Ren Zhengfei's little daughter was a fan of Steve Jobs. When Jobs died, he mourned with his daughter for a minute as a father.

On 31 December 1999, Ren Zhengfei intended to visit his mother in Kunming. Unfortunately, his mother had a car accident on her way back from grocery shopping. Not long after, Ren Zhengfei went to see her and she died. His father died in 1995.

In the article *My father, My Mother*, Ren Zhengfei wrote:

"I always thought my mother was in good health, and there would be a lot of time. My health was not good, and my knowledge and ability would eventually fall behind, when I would quit the company and go to accompany her. I didn't expect misfortune. Looking back on my history, I searched my conscience and found myself not in debt to my country or my people, my employees or my friends. The only people I was indebted to were my parents. I didn't take care of them in their bad situation, nor in my good situation.

"Dad, Mom, no matter how many times I called you, you couldn't hear. The dead are gone. Those of us who are alive need to move on."

In his self-introduction, Ren Zhengfei said that he was an indoors person – going home straight after work, reading or watching TV shows or documentaries. One of his favourite books was A Message to Garcia by Elbert Hubbard, published 100 years ago. He listed it as a must-read to cultivate employees' dedication.

He also thought about his life after retirement. He would say that once he left work, he would open a bottle of champagne in celebration. He might even open a café or a restaurant, or run a personal farm.

In the spring festival of 2013, Ericsson released its fourth quarter and annual financial reports; their sales revenue was 35.3 billion USD for 2013. The annual sales revenue for Huawei was about 238 to 240 billion RMB, equivalent to

39.3 to 39.6 billion USD; this was the first time that Huawei had beaten Ericsson in annual sales revenue and ascended to the throne of the biggest telecom manufacturer in the world. Mr Hans Vestberg, the CEO of Ericsson said: "We respect such rivalry with Huawei."

The vice president for domestic terminals and the CMO of Huawei said that as the era of 1G belonged to Motorola, 2G to Nokia and 3G to Apple and Samsung, the era of 4G would be dominated by Huawei. A report on the NetEase Finance Channel glorified Huawei, mentioning that if Huawei didn't exist, residents in Siberia wouldn't be connected; hikers at the Kilimanjaro Volcano couldn't send out rescue signals. It explained that even telecom providers in Paris, London and Sydney used Huawei's base transceiver stations to serve you after you landed. Huawei's presence has spread to Mount Everest, 8,000 kilometres above sea level, the frozen North Pole and South Pole below -40 °C, and the impoverished lands in Africa.

Huawei's headquarters in the Banxuegang Industrial Zone, Longgang, Shenzhen cover an area of 200,000 square kilometres, the largest of its type in Shenzhen. Ren Zhengfei used to question that: "Lin Zhiling is beautiful. Why can't we make Huawei's industrial zone as beautiful?" After much attentive effort, the grounds were covered with the shade of green trees and the aroma of plants, and a shimmering man-made lake was centred in the park.

In this beautiful garden–industrial zone, you would not have thought its owner would keep a humble appearance by his casual dress. If you met him, you would probably think he was an ordinary senior, rather than the president of Huawei, who had been inflicted with depression, diabetes and cancer surgery.

At an international consulting conference, Ren Zhengfei said: "I didn't have any connections with government officers personally, nor entrepreneurs. Except for a little contact with Liu Chuanzhi and Wangzhi, my personal life was very lonely and grievous. I kept a distance from ordinary employees to maintain checks and balances, and endured my solitary state."

Ren Zhengfei was thrust into the spotlight and experienced too much pressure. With regard to the "Chinese Dream" to rise up in international business, and for independent domestic telecoms development, Ren Zhengfei had, "Broken through tangible barriers, fluttered and soared to great achievements, weathered storms and frosts, blazed trails and broken paths for Huawei."

APPENDICES

MY FATHER, MY MOTHER

On the last day of the last century, my conscience finally pricked me. After a business trip, I bought a flight ticket from Beijing to Kunming to go to see my mother. I did not give her a call when getting my ticket, because I knew she would toil the whole afternoon to make the type of food that I liked in childhood. Not until the plane was ready to take off, did I call her. I told her not to bother other people or send cars to pick me up. I would take a taxi home, and all I wanted was to spend some time with her. A few years ago, I used to visit my mother every year, but would be picked up by our Kunming office right after getting off the plane. They would always introduce this important customer to meet with or that important customer to have dinner with. Running around, I only saw my parents just before I left, picking up luggage from home and bidding them goodbye. After all the delays, day and night, my mom's hope of some family time always came to nothing, but they always said to me: "Your work is important. You take care of your work first."

Due to my scheduled visit in Iran with vice president Hu Jintao, I could only spend one day in Kunming and needed to get back to Beijing by the 3rd. I told my mom about vice premier Wu Bangguo's half-hour talk with me during the visit to Africa last November. He told me that it was his idea to let me join him on that visit, for three purposes: first, it was encouragement and praise for Huawei, and a chance for Huawei to be known and understood directly by other ministers on the journey; second, he wanted to know how

Huawei was operated and managed, to see if there were some lessons that could be applied to other enterprises; third, he wanted to check how the government could help Huawei to expand in the international market. My mom was pleased to hear this and said: "Thanks to the trust of the government, as long as Huawei is running well, rumours will shatter over the course of time."

In recent years, many opinions and speculations have pervaded the media and online, criticism and accolade alike. Living in the shadow of the Cultural Revolution, my mom was not interested in praise, but was concerned by some articles that didn't know the real situation at Huawei. I told her that we were not a listed company, and didn't need to publicize our track record to society. We were held accountable for the sufficient operation of the company and administrative regulations. We didn't want to repudiate every comment about Huawei. The newspaper columns were too valuable to be used for debate over our small company. We didn't want to be held responsible for distracting from the government propaganda focus. Some people didn't understand us, and we didn't explain. When they understood, things would improve. My mom sighed with relief. She understood my silence. I also made a pact with my mom that I would not work or go on business trips during the spring festival that year, and I would accompany her to Hainan with my brothers and sisters to have a nice holiday, and we would have a blast chatting with each other. Before that, I always went abroad to secure some working time since other countries don't celebrate Chinese festivals. I was awakening now to the realization that I should spend more time with my mom. I had never spent much time with her. However, I did not get the chance.

On the 8th, we successfully finished our visit to Iran. We had just seen vice-president Hu off at the airport when I got a phone call from Ji Ping. He told me that my mom was hit by a car around 10 o'clock in the morning when she left the grocery market, with two small bags of groceries in her hands, and GM Sun had gone to Kunming to handle the hospital coordination. A thousand miles away, with bad phone reception, I was burning with anxiety. I needed a few transfers to get back. The layover in Balin was six and a half hours, a real torture for me. The flight was two hours late in Balin due to thunderstorms, and another ten minutes late in Bangkok. I could not catch the flight to Kunming in time. When I arrived in Kunming, it was already midnight.

As soon as I got there, I knew my mom wouldn't pull through. Her head was severely injured. Machines and medicine maintained her heartbeat and breathing. They did not tell me over the phone for the fear that I would have an accident on the way. I saw my mom lying in peace on the hospital bed, free from labours and worries, like having the rest she had never had in life.

I truly regretted that I hadn't given her a call while I was in Iran. On the 7th, vice president Hu met the eight entrepreneurs in the visiting group, including me. I gave a report for two to three minutes. When I introduced myself from Huawei, vice president Hu held up four fingers, signifying that we are one of the four big national companies. I wanted to call my mom to tell her the good news that the national leader knew Huawei, but I refrained, because every time I called my mom, home and abroad, she would always nag me: "You are on a business trip again." "Feifei, your body condition is no better than mine." "Feifei, you have more wrinkles than I do." "Feifei, you can't walk any better than I can." "Feifei, banquets will make your diabetes worse. Your heart is not in a good condition." I thought to myself that my mom would not stop nagging me if I called her from Iran, such a bad living environment. I would see her in a few days, so I did not call her, which became the biggest regret in my life. Due to the time difference, I could only call her on the morning of the 8th to tell her the news. If my call had delayed her for a minute or two, she might have escaped from the accident. I can't express how regretful I feel.

My mom passed away soon after I got to the hospital and I caught a last glimpse of her. My father died on the streets of Kunming too. He bought a drink in a plastic package from a street vendor and suffered from diarrhoea until major organ failure ended his life.

My father, Ren Moxun, working hard through his life, at best was deemed as a countryside educator. My mother, Cheng Yuanzhao, was the most ordinary type of teacher, who accompanied my father in a shared life career of educating underprivileged children in mountainous areas.

In a land reform brigade winter uniform, my father, together with PLA bandits suppressing troops, went to an ethnic minority inhabited mountainous area in Guizhou to build a middle school. Many years passed by before he returned. Quite a few of his students became senior cadres of the party and the state, and some even became leaders of national universities and colleges, but my father was still a humble countryside teacher.

My grandfather was a master at curing ham in Pujiang, Zhejiang. None of my father's brothers or sisters went to school. My grandfather felt guilty, and my father constantly requested he went to school. During his school years in Beijing, my father was an ardent youth, participating in student movements, delivering anti-Japanese speeches, campaigning against the Tanaka Memorial and joining the Communist Youth League. Since my grandparents died in quick succession, my father dropped out of school one year away from graduation and went home. It was the start of the first KMT-CPC Cooperation and the prelude of anti-Japanese culmination. With a introduction by some country folks, my father went to be an accountant in a Kuomintang military factory in Guangzhou since the director was from his hometown too. The imminent danger of war moved the factory to Rongshui, Guangxi, and later Tongzi, Guizhou. While in Rongshui, Guangxi, my father opened a bookstore with some of his friends to sell revolutionary books. He also organized a book club, "July 7th", which drove dozens of people to the front line of the revolution, and many of them became senior cadres in the party and country. After smashing the Gang of Four, party history was rewritten and my father was invited to his role in Rongshui.

This event induced the biggest tribulation for my father during the Cultural Revolution. He had worked for Kuomintang's military factory. Though he advocated the anti-Japanese war and came on board with Communist Party policies, he did not contact the underground Communist Party organization. What was the reason? It was because he doubted some people. How could that be explained in the climate of the Cultural Revolution?

My mother, on the other hand, only received a high school education. She accompanied my father to endure all sorts of humiliation. She sheltered my father from more afflictions and took care of me and my six siblings. As soon as she put down the chalk at work, she picked up briquettes, untiringly engaged in the duty of getting groceries, cooking and laundry. She also needed to educate herself up to the task of teaching. Eventually, she became a senior teacher. Among her students, many grew to be excellent technical experts at the provincial or municipal level, who held the impression of my mother's hard work. The long journey my mother had taken to counteract her inadequate formal education was only known to herself.

Although my parents joined the revolution early, they were not proletariat descendants. To earn the trust and blend in with the proletarian revolutionary force was not a simple thing for them. They were not regarded as pure revolutionists like farmers or workers. A complicated and diverse society could not consist of only one pure matter. In each political movement, they opened their hearts to the party. Their way of ideological reforms was made much harder, and their inner torment was not obvious to everyone. They recounted their life in profound detail for system evaluation. After they passed away, I asked an old school mate to help copy their profiles. He burst into tears after reading their materials. They followed the revolution throughout their lives. Though not regarded as hardcore revolutionaries, they didn't demean the Party or the people. My father finally joined the Party in 1958 when the Party absorbed high intellectuals. To open up heart-to-heart was not as easy as in the information age nowadays. To disagree with individual party members could be depicted as anti-party. We watched our parents live with timid and overcautious minds, and dedicate to their work with no extra attention for us, just as I worked too hard to spare any time for them. Their loyalty to their careers, to the Party and to the country is mirrored in history. What I want to confess today is my negligence for not spending more time with them.

In retrospect, hardcore revolutionaries were minorities. They fought fearlessly and selflessly in the name of the revolution and became pillars of society. It was worth the cost of more investigation to identify these minorities. People like my parents, who followed the revolution, supported the revolution, or at least were not on the opposite side of revolution were the majority. They were much better than the anti-revolutionaries. Society should accept such people and give them a chance, rather than demand their pure devotion or spend so much time on investigating them, which inflicted them with endless pain. Ideological pursuits should develop together with a material foundation. The material foundation should consolidate ideological achievements, a mechanism to motivate people working for the quality of life, while working for the revolution unconsciously, which prompted their enthusiasm to full play. After I presided over Huawei, we had lax rules for our employees or former employees, while setting a high bar for management cadres. Only those who were hardworking, dedicated, responsible and motivated individuals were qualified to join in the cadre's teams. My experience with the remolding ideology of my parents shaped my tolerance.

The deepest impression from my youth was the difficult time during the Three Year Natural Disasters with my parents, which is still vivid in my mind.

I have six siblings, and a big family of nine, entirely reliant on my parents' meagre salaries. As hard as it was, it became even more difficult as my siblings and I grew up, with the need for new clothes and school tuition to pay. The two to three kuai tuition for each semester was a great expense for my family, worrying my mom every time. The situation got worse for my family compared to those families whose salaries could make ends meet. I always saw my mom attempting to borrow three to five kuai at the end of each month to feed the family – this was sometimes futile after a few tries. I never wore a shirt until high school graduation. Some classmates, seeing me in a heavy coat in hot weather, would suggest I ask my mom for a shirt. I would never do that. I knew it was impossible. When I went to university, my mom gave me two shirts. I choked up, because I knew my new shirts would make life even harder for my siblings. Two or three of us shared a quilt, with bundles of straws below the sheet. When rebel factions searched our house and confiscated our properties during the Cultural Revolution, they were astonished by how little we possessed as a family of high level intellectuals and a former school principal. That I needed to take a bed sheet with me to university aggravated the situation because of the quota system for cotton and cloth, which limited the consumption of cloth to a minimum of 0.5 metres per person per year. To make me a sheet, my mom picked up a few old ones discarded by graduates, cleaned them, sewed patches and stitched a bed sheet for me, which accompanied me for my five years at university in Chongqing.

My parents were not selfish at all, which was perceivable in the situation of the day. I was fourteen to fifteen years old and the eldest child. My siblings were young and innocent. My parents could have sneaked a mouthful more of food for themselves, but they never did that. My father sometimes had a conference to go to where he would have some good food, but my humble mother, undertaking the same amount of work and carrying the burden to feed and raise seven children, consumed herself in all kinds of chores, cooking, laundry and fixing the stove, and never ate a mouthful of more food. We stringently served individual portions each meal, to control our hunger for food, and ensure everyone could live. Otherwise, one or two of my younger siblings would not survive. I truly understood that.

When I was studying for a big exam in the senior year of high school, sometimes in unbearable hunger, I mixed rice bran and vegetables in a batter and made pancakes. My father noticed this a few times and it made him upset. In fact, we were too destitute back then to have a lockable cabinet, but I dared not grab a handful of rice in the crock, for fear that one or two of my brothers or sisters would die of starvation. (I learned to be selfless from my parents. The success of Huawei could be attributed to my selflessness in some regards.) In the last three months before the exam, my mom always gave me a small piece of corn bread in the morning, to settle my stomach for the days' study. The small piece of corn bread should be given the credit for enabling me to pass the university entrance tests. If not, I wouldn't have made it to Huawei. There would be one more pig-raising expert or street craftsman. The little piece of corn bread was scraped from my parents and my siblings' meal, something I could never reciprocate.

In the higher education reform in 1997, universities started to charge tuition from students, while no student loans were provided. Huawei donated 25 million RMB fund to the Ministry of Education to support underprivileged students.

As cautious as my father was, aware of his background, buried in academics and never speaking up in any situation, he was still doomed. He was taken as a reactionary academic authority, capitalist roader, and one with historical problems in the movements of getting rid of evil people of all kinds during the Cultural Revolution. He was among the first few to be imprisoned in a cow barn.

In 1967, fierce violent conflicts took over Chongqing. I snuck on a train to get home. I got beaten up by a Shanghai rebel faction because I didn't have a ticket. They didn't allow me to pay upon arrival and kicked me off the train. I was beaten up again in the railway station by the railway staff. When I finally took the train home, I dared not get off at my home stop but a stop earlier, and walked a dozen li home. I arrived home at midnight. My parents didn't have the time to express their heartache, but let me go the next morning for fear that the implication would inflict my future. My father took off his pair of old shoes to give to me. Before I left the next morning, my father said a few words to me: "Remember, knowledge is power. While others give up, you have to keep learning. Don't go with the stream. Help your younger siblings when you are capable." With this trust, I settled myself to go over the advanced mathematics exercises Fan Yingchuan had compiled twice under a hail of bullets in Chongqing, and taught myself logic, philosophy and three foreign languages to the level of reading college textbooks. I was not a language genius. I forgot most of them after having no place to apply them for twenty years in the military. I wore the shoes my father gave me, without realizing that he needed them more for his laborious work in muddy water, cold and wet. Looking back, I feel I was too selfish.

My family's economic situation became even more arduous during the Cultural Revolution compared to the natural disaster period. In order to crack down the financial foundation of capitalist roaders, the central revolution government issued a living standard of less than 15 yuan per person per month, which was scraped again by each level of rebel faction, leaving only 10 yuan for each person. A college friend of mine worked in the sub-district office, and introduced my brothers and sisters to work digging sand in the river or carrying earth for the earthwork in railway repair projects. My siblings chipped in 100 yuan for me when I got married, which was made from the suffering of sifting sand in icy cold water and the risks of being buried under the collapse of earthwork. We could endure the hard life, but the torture of the mind was more agonizing. In the wake of my father's background checks, my brothers and sisters were deprived of higher education again and again, even if they passed the entrance tests each time. Except for me, who was a junior college student when the Cultural Revolution started, my siblings didn't even finish a high school, middle school or elementary school education. Their essential life skills were self-taught afterwards. Looking back now, the hardships and spiritual torments became valuable treasures in our life.

The Cultural Revolution was a national catastrophe, a server test in life. It made me politically mature, no longer a simple nerd. I also participated in the vigorous Red Guards movement, but I was not a Red Guard, a startling scene at that time. Because of my father's background check ups, no Red Guards branch accepted me.

After I was enlisted, my application to join the Party was not approved because of my father's problems, until the crackdown of the Gang of Four.

In October 1976, the Central Committee smashed the Gang of Four and liberated us from background problems. Suddenly I became an awards reaper. No matter how hard I tried, I had no chance to be rewarded for meritorious actions during the Cultural Revolution. Under my leadership, my soldiers were awarded with Third Class Merits, Second Class Merits and Collective Third Class Merits, except me, who was never awarded with merits. I had been accustomed to a quiet life without awards or attention, which became the foundation of my indifference to honours now. After the crack down on the Gang of Four, my life changed completely. Two of my inventions filled scientific gaps nationwide, and my technical innovation was needed over time. Suddenly, the honour of 'Hero' and 'Model' flooded towards me from all directions, from the military as well as local governments. I was not prone to ecstasy. The awards I received were assigned to others.

In March 1978, I attended the National Science Conference. Among the 6,000 attendees, only 150 were under the age of 35. I was 33 years old. I was also one of the few non-Party representatives from the military line. Under the solicitude of the military party committee, people were send out to investigate my father's background before the vindication, repudiate the false claims about my father and sent their findings to the local organization. I finally joined the Party, and attended the 12th National Congress of CPC later. My father made a large frame for the picture I took with central Party leaders, and hung it up as an honour to my whole family.

My father was vindicated soon after the capture of the Gang of Four. Everything needed to be restored at that time. The Party needed to rehabilitate some top high schools and improve the admission rate of universities and colleges. My father was appointed to be a middle school principal. Before the Cultural Revolution, my father was the president of a vocational college. He didn't care about the level of the position or personal gains or losses, and threw himself into the work tirelessly. The quality of teaching improved, and the college entrance rate rose to over 90%. His school gained a reputation far and wide. He retired at the age of 75 in 1984. He said he caught up at the end of life and did something. He wished for us to appreciate the time we have and make good use of it. We've parted since then, each focused on our work. I was proud of the older generation for their political morality. After they were released from the cow barn, and returned back to normal life, they spared no effort at work, never disturbed by personal gains or losses, honour or indignity, patriotic and loyal to the Party and their careers, which set models to teach our generation, the next generation, and generations to come. We can't live our lives without setbacks, but our will to fight for the people will not waver.

I had the privilege to meet Mr Luo Ruiqing three months before he died when he spoke on behalf of the military at the National Scientific Conference. He said the next few decades would be an extraordinary peaceful period for us and to invest fully in economic construction. I was young and lacking political vision, and didn't understand what he meant. Two or three years later, the disarmament cut off the whole line of our arm of services, when I started to understand the prescience of leaders.

After I transferred to civilian work, I couldn't adapt to the market economy, nor manage to survive in it. I tumbled in a managing position at an electronics company and suffered as a victim of a scam. I found Huawei because I had no other choices, and the first few years of starting up were difficult, with my parents, my nephew and me crammed into a house that was a dozen square metres, and using the balcony as a makeshift kitchen. My parents worried about me all the time, and lived parsimoniously to save some money to bail me out when needed. My younger sister told me, a few months before her death, my mom told her that she saved ten thousand yuan for me just in case my business failed. When she was hit by the car, she only had a few dozen kuai with her, and no identity card. She was rescued by a 110 ambulance as a nobody. Not until lunch time, when my sister and her husband found she hadn't returned, did they find out about the car accident. Poor parents. A mother's heart could be as pure as this. When we lived in Guangdong, fish and shrimp became much cheaper when they were dead. My parents would buy dead fish and shrimp specifically, claiming it was much more tender than the meat inland. They went grocery shopping at night because things were cheaper after they did not sell out during the day. I didn't have the time to take care of them, so much so that I was unaware of my mom's serious diabetes and was told by a neighbour. After Huawei scaled up in development, I was faced with the huge task of management adaption. I didn't take care of either my parents or myself. My health was crushed at that time. It was then that my parents moved to Kunming to live with my younger sister. I then understood the sacrifice required to pursue excellence. The success of Huawei had cost me the responsibility and opportunity to take care of my parents and my personal health.

Looking back at my history, I have searched my conscience and found myself not owing to my country or my people, my employees or my friends. The only people I have been indebted to are my parents. I didn't take care of them when they were in a bad situation nor when I was in a good situation.

Dad, Mom, no matter how many times I called you, you couldn't hear.

The dead are gone. Those of us who are alive need to move on.

8 Feburary 2001, Shenzhen

XINHUA NEWS INTERVIEW, REN ZHENGFEI: CHARGING ONE FORT FOR 28 YEARS

In 1987, the 43 year-old Ren Zhengfei, together with five partners, raised 21,000 RMB and registered the company Huawei. They started up with two multimetres and an oscilloscope in a desolate shack in Shenzhen.

In 28 years, Huawei has developed from a small obscure workshop into a global telecom leader, whose sales revenue in 2015 reached 395 billion RMB, with a net profit of 36.9 billion RMB and an annual increase of over 30%. As the pioneering leader of Huawei, Ren Zhengfei has transformed from a middle-aged start up businessman to a world-renowned entrepreneur, and impacted many lives.

What paths has Huawei crossed in the spirit of entrepreneurship and innovation? What is its success code? What is the only focus Ren Zhengfei engaged in for 28 years? What's the journey like? How can we drive new innovations in Shenzhen and China, in his opinion? What protection dams does the government need to reinforce?

On 5 March 2016, Xinhua news reporters went to Huawei headquarters in Longgang, Shenzhen, to have a face-to-face conversation for over three hours, to find answers to a series of questions.

THE SUCCESS CODE: "TO FOCUS ON ONE MATTER"

Reporter: Huawei's business has soared against the gloomy outlook of the global economy. What's the innate gene and secret to Huawei's success?

Ren Zhengfei: Firstly, the development of Huawei benefited from changes in the national political climate and economic environment in Shenzhen. If not for the reform and opening up policy, there would be no Huawei. In 1987 Document No.18 in Shenzhen clarified the rights for private enterprise property. Without this document, we could not have founded Huawei. Later, after Huawei developed to a certain degree, when we started to feel the heavy burden of taxes and fees, many colleagues of mine proposed dividing the money and ending the company. Right then, the Shenzhen government issued 22 regulations, to introduce no tax obligations for investment until the enterprise started to make profit. It lasted for a few years, which prompted us to grow in sales.

Secondly, Huawei persisted for 28 years only in the field of telecoms and charged the forts relentlessly. After our initial development, we focused on one matter, to expand in one field. When we only had a dozen people, we charged the forts in this field. It remained the same when we grew to a few hundred and gained a few thousand employees, and even to tens of tens of thousands of people, which guaranteed intensive gunfire and saturated attacks. We dedicated over 100 billion yuan every year to the forts in this field, among which R&D took up 60 billion and market service took up around 50-60 billion yuan. Ultimately, we led the world in data transmission, when we started to advocate the establishment of a new order in an open and win-win frame, constructive for an information society encompassing tens of thousands of enterprises worldwide.

Thirdly, Huawei is unswervingly engaged in reform and learning from western business operations. We spent 28 years learning from western business management and have not yet completed the process. Compared with some companies, our management is good enough, but we hire 20,000 more management staff and cost 4 billion USD more in management expenditures than mature multinational companies like Ericsson. We are constantly optimizing the organization and processes to enhance internal efficiency.

Reporter: Huawei spends hundreds of millions of USD every year for IBM management consulting. Why does Huawei spend so much on improving management?

Ren Zhengfei: Did you know that a retired Toyota board member led a senior staff team to work for us for 10 years, and a German team from a research institute worked in Huawei for over ten years too? The combined effort made our production process scientific and standardized. From products costing tens of thousands of RMB to ones worth tens of billions of USD, Huawei grew better, because we paid billions of USD on consulting.

When we stepped out of the country to the world platform, we knew nothing, not even about the delivery. We counted on the help of engineering consultants from all over the world. The first thing we needed to do was to learn and standardize company management. Now we are progressing and pursuing simpler and better management.

Reporter: Does Huawei have a blind side?

Ren Zhengfei: Yes. Huawei was on the edge of collapse three years ago. Why? Because staff were getting rich and could not tolerate bitterness. We couldn't find people to work overseas voluntarily. They wanted to buy a house, and stay with their kids in a better environment in Beijing. We started to ponder: Why don't we raise the compensation and benefits for people working on the front line? We made sure that 'generals' in Africa had different standards than workers in Beijing and Shanghai. Young people could rise to become a general very soon in Africa. If they worked in Africa, their goal would be to become a general and receive the corresponding pay. Now our staff in Africa don't even want to come back.

Reporter: What kind of future will innovation lead Huawei to?

Ren Zhengfei: For example, the 4k high definition television – neither Beijing nor Shenzhen could achieve that – but it was available for the whole Sichuan province, including rural areas, which was our cooperation project with a Sichuan telecom company. 4k high definition TV would largely expand the bandwidth and information pipeline. Cellphones are going to enter the 2k age, and expand the information pipeline too. There must be someone responsible for such a big pipe. While the 4k age has not arrived yet, virtual reality is imminent. The traffic for VR and interactive activities is going to be far greater than 4K. It is an inevitable trend as well as a strategic opportunity. It could be in the market for Hong Kong and Macao soon. The practice in Sichuan proved the countryside areas could enjoy high speed broadband too.

HOLD THE GROUND OF "SANGGAMNYONG": 'THE FOCUS OF IDEALS'

Reporter: Huawei's development coincided with the outburst of the domestic real estate market. Has your mind been stirred?

Ren Zhengfei: No. We have never been into the stock market or real estate market.

Reporter: Have you been lured by it?

Ren Zhengfei: No. There was a stock exchange downstairs in our building, where people involved in the stock business were crowded, layers around layers. In contrast, the upstairs was as calm as a lake and people were engaged in work. We were focused on one thing – to charge the fort.

Reporter: How has this culture been cultivated?

Ren Zhengfei: To be foolish and not revolve around money. The focus was on ideals to hold the ground of Sanggamnyng. Money was not crucial.

Reporter: Why doesn't Huawei go public?

Ren Zhengfei: Because we are not crazy about profits. We are working hard for ideals and ambitions. To hold the ground of Sanggamnyng was hard, incurring many sacrifices. If we went public, shareholders would push us horizontally into the lucrative stock market for billions or tens of billions profit, and we couldn't march into the 'no people land'.

THE INNOVATOR'S DILEMMA: "EVEN IF THERE IS A 'BLACK SWAN', IT WOULD BE IN OUR COFFEE CUP."

Reporter: A lot of big companies have collapsed overnight throughout history, as depicted in The Innovator's Dilemma. Do you have such concerns?

Ren Zhengfei: At least it won't happen in the field of big data transmission. Even if there is a black swan, it would be in our coffee cup, granting us time to transfer the 'black swan' to a 'white swan'. We are very open and liberal inside. The black swan would only appear in our coffee cup, rather than outside. We have become the culmination of advanced technology trends.

Reporter: You are optimistic about Huawei's future, but why do you keep asking "Whether Huawei is the next to fall apart?"

Ren Zhengfei: I have two points. Firstly, we may cut ourselves some slack. After fast development, are we going to become lethargic? We need to recognize our weaknesses. Secondly, our country needs to reinforce the protection of intellectual properties. Property is protected by real rights law, as should be intellectual property. Intellectual property right protection will give birth to innovation.

Reporter: Has Huawei signed a patent cross license agreement with Ericsson not long ago?

Ren Zhengfei: Yes. Senior management cheered at signing such an agreement, because we bought a world access ticket. An ordinary staff member wrote a post on-line, "We are shaking hands with the world. The world is in our hands." If we protect innovation and invention, many people would go on to pursue original ideas, which could develop into big industries.

BROADEN THE CHANNEL: "THE MAIN CHANNEL WILL KEEP GETTING BROADER, MUCH MORE THAN YOU CAN IMAGINE."

Reporter: The competition is ferocious, but you just mentioned the open conversation with foreign competitors. How did you manage that? Was there not a scorched earth policy for competitors?

Ren Zhengfei: Other people may engage in the scorched earth policy, but we never did. Even as a small company in the beginning, Huawei was open and friendly. How do we have such a good place in the international market? Because the 'nuclear umbrella' for intellectual property rights has been built up. For many years, we paid for access to other intellectual property rights, and we charged for use of our own intellectual properties. To sign a patent cross license agreement with different corporations was essentially a gesture of friendship and respect. Now we have developed further in the industry. We should care about the overall development across the world.

Reporter: Huawei always battles in the main channel. Has the main channel become broader or thinner? Have competitors become more and stronger? What's the situation like?

Ren Zhengfei: The main channel will keep getting broader, much more than you can imagine. I couldn't have foreseen the information society we live in today. We just broadened the channel, on which yachts, cargo ships or wooden boats could sail, and we charged the toll for the course. We need to build cooperation with thousands of enterprises to achieve this goal.

CONTROL THE 'TWO DAMS': "THE GOVERNMENT WAS MAINLY RESPONSIBLE FOR SETTING UP THE RULES."

Reporter: How is the relationship with the government or enterprises in Shenzhen? Do you have any suggestions for the government?

Ren Zhengfei: Shenzhen city government has done very well in not interfering with specific business operations. As long as the government controls the two dams of legal regulation and market-oriented policy, they should leave enterprises to operate themselves inside the dam. The major responsibility for governments is to set up rules and provide effective support in legal and market terms.

Reporter: How does the innovative economy of Shenzhen take the lead across the country?

Ren Zhengfei: Shenzhen is at the forefront for legalization and marketization. The court would make fair decisions in intellectual property lawsuits.

Reporter: In past years, the Pearl River delta region was known as the 'world factory'. How do you perceive the development path for the world factory, the Pearl River Delta? What's its value for innovation development and innovation drive?

Ren Zhengfei: If you had come to Huawei twenty years ago, you would have thought Huawei was going to go bankrupt very soon. We started the company in a desolate shack with two multimetres and a single oscilloscope. We used to lag behind, worse than manufacturing factories in the Pearl River delta.

Evolution is a step-by-step process. Now a large number of labour-intensive industries in the Pearl River delta have transferred to Southeast Asia. You cannot just view the success of a few high-tech companies in the Pearl River delta separately. They grew from a 'low-tech' base. If conditions permit, a low-tech business can improve, exceed itself and evolve slowly. High-tech companies also need components and parts from the low-tech.

Reporter: That means without the manufacturing industry, there would be no foundation to develop high-tech companies?

Ren Zhengfei: Yes. How many low-tech contributions are involved in high-tech products? Can every single component and part be high tech? No. How many components and parts comprise our products? We used to pay RMB for those components and pick them up in Dongguan. Now we need to pay USD and pick them up in southeast Asia.

WAY TO PROSPERITY:
"A SPADE MUST BE USED TO PLANT CORN.
CORN IS THE ENTITY OF BUSINESS."

Reporter: What do you think the focus should be in expanding the reform and opening up practices if we are to seize the opportunity?

Ren Zhengfei: Firstly, tax reduction. Tax cuts will continuously relieve the burden of enterprises and thereby increase investment in research and innovation. With money directed to research, enterprises will gain the space for rehabilitation and catching up. The industry will grow bigger and, in turn, increase the tax base. Secondly, to reform the distribution mechanism between labour and capital. The distribution between labour and capital has maintained a ratio of 3:1 at Huawei for all these years. To set a distribution ratio between capital and labour for the annual increased value each year could mobilize the initiative of workers.

Reporter: What's the relationship between innovation and reform?

Ren Zhengfei: Innovation means to emancipate productivity, and create a concrete value for the sake of a nation's prosperity. Virtual economy serves as a tool, like a hoe. To own fifty or more hoes does not mean anything unless they serve the purpose of planting corn. Corn is the business entity. We still have to develop the entity enterprises, centred on satisfying people's material and cultural needs, to stabilize society.

Reporter: Some people say the reform momentum has been waning in recent years. What's your opinion?

Ren Zhengfei: I think if everyone holds an illusion to make a great fortune overnight, it can't be achieved, and thus momentum declines. In fact, Heaven and Earth do not pass away and the countryside view of a windlass, fences and dogs doesn't change either. How could you become the 'affluent second generation'? If we embrace a mindset of working hard and developing gradually, everyone's satisfaction will multiply.

STRATEGIC PATIENCE:
"INNOVATION WITH NO THEORETICAL
UNDERPINNING COULDN'T LAST, NOR SUCCEED."

Reporter: Silicon Valley is the global high-tech highland. What's the hope for Chinese innovation?

Ren Zhengfei: The crucial matter in the high-tech field is concentration. With innovation, yet without theoretical underpinning, it is impossible to create a large industry. "One needs to sit on the cold bench for ten years," and even longer, for the theoretical bench. In scientific research, people are more important than equipment. A simple piece of equipment can bring in complicated research results, but simple-minded people can't achieve anything, even with the most advanced equipment.

Reporter: Can other 'Huaweis' be cultivated in China?

Ren Zhengfei: Yes. Firstly, small enterprises need to focus on customer service for development. Small enterprises, especially start-ups, need to dedicate to serious, accountable and sincere customer service. Small enterprises don't need to care too much about methodology. Like grinding tofu – good tofu will sell out. Be sincere with customers and improve services, and they will have the chance. Don't complicate company management at this stage. Secondly, focus on one field, persistent to be a 'screw'. Thirdly, small enterprises should ward off ego inflation after initial success. I believe enterprises should develop step by step.

Economy bubbles are destructive to China. We must engage in scientific research with a down-to-earth attitude.

That a basic theory developed into a large industry would take decades of effort. We must have strategic patience. We need to respect scientists, who are engaged in research. If bubbles prevail in academic research, a high-tech future for China is going to be difficult. No bubbles, no worry, no leap forward. Innovation with no theoretical underpinning will not last, nor succeed.

Our company has established more than twenty competence centres in places where world resources are gathered. Without theoretical breakthroughs from these centres, we would not have achieved our position in the world. China needs to focus on theoretical breakthroughs, to pave the path for innovation. Small-scale reforms cannot make a big industry.

Reporter: Does theoretical innovation refer to fundamental research?

Ren Zhengfei: Theoretical innovation is even ahead of fundamental research, since the equation cannot be understood by anyone, just like the theory of relativity written by Einstein could not be understood a hundred years ago. After a hundred years' study, scientists proved it right. Many a breakthrough theory cannot be understood by people of its time.

Reporter: Has Huawei employed many foreign scientists?

Ren Zhengfei: Many scientists are foreigners in our overseas research institutes. Directors are Chinese and their job is to serve the scientists. In the '2012 lab', we have 700 scientists now, which will be increased to over 1,400 this year.

Reporter: Should high-tech development be supported by fundamental theory?

Ren Zhengfei: Only fundamental theory can produce a thriving industry and technical innovation will push us forward too. A small screw factory in Japan perfected the production over dozens of years. The screws they produced would never come loose, and are used by high-speed railways across the world. There are many things to research about a little screw. I have been to many village factories in Germany that manufacture one product for dozens of years. Their promotion publication does not list how much they have sold, but their percentage in the world market. They are village factories.

Reporter: Based on your experience in Huawei's growth, how can we 'seize' a share of high-tech development in the next economic cycle?

Ren Zhengfei: First, don't use the concept of 'seize'. To seize something can induce a lot of bubbles. We need to concentrate on building a solid foundation, integrating into the world trend, developing together with others and sharing the world's success.

IN THE NEXT 30 YEARS:
"MANY BIG INDUSTRIES WILL EMERGE."

Reporter: Many people say one driving factor behind Shenzhen's innovation development path is Huawei?

Ren Zhengfei: The depth and span of an information society cannot be imagined. Massive changes will happen to human society in the next twenty to thirty years. With the breakthrough of biotechnology, and the realization of artificial intelligence, many new industries will emerge in society.

We are facing a great challenge in intellectual property rights. The past two or three decades was the time to advance to broadband communications. A great number of big companies emerged around the world: Cisco, Google, Facebook, Apple. There were not many in China, because of the inadequate protection of intellectual properties. Many big industries will emerge in the future, such as the VR industry, where China has advantages, but for better development we need to take serious measures for the protection of intellectual property.

Reporter: What kind of business environment do you think China should build up and maintain?

Ren Zhengfei: I think the 'New Norm' proposed by the central government is correct. We are not pursuing a rate of development right now. We need to slow down and concentrate on the quality of development.

An expert has said that there are two kinds of investments: one is to expand, like to build up steel factories one after another until scaling up; the other is the 'Prometheus' act. Prometheus stole fire for human civilization. This is the innovation breakthrough. Our government proposed to develop the economy by increasing innovation. It is absolutely correct. Expanding development won't achieve the ideal results of a price drop due to the glut of the same products.

Reporter: In your opinion, as we are embracing unprecedented opportunities, what are the biggest risks?

Ren Zhengfei: I think the Chinese economy does not have such huge problems as we imagined, as long as we don't produce bubbles. The situation in China is better than in other countries. As long as we don't have rampant fake products, there won't be big problems.

PREVENTING THE CRISIS: "HIGH COSTS WILL EVENTUALLY DESTROY YOUR COMPETITIVENESS."

Reporter: In your opinion, what's the crisis for Shenzhen in the future?

Ren Zhengfei: It's very simple. One hundred and forty years ago, the centre of the world was Pittsburgh because of the steel industry. Seventy years ago, the centre of the world was Detroit because of automobiles. Now, where is the centre of the world? I don't know. It's been decentralized. Capital will fly to low cost places. High costs will eventually destroy your competitiveness. The high-speed railway network, the information system and highway webs evoked and formed a dynamic distribution system, which won't gather in high cost places.

Reporter: Huawei is a local enterprise of Shenzhen. What's your expectation of the city development in Shenzhen in terms of globalization, reform and opening up, etc.?

Ren Zhengfei: Shenzhen has developed too much in real estate, and fallen short of industrial land. We know in the development of big industry, each company needs some physical space.

Our country will eventually move towards industrial modernization. Industrial modernization is the most important among the four modernizations. Land needs to be provided for industrial growth. As land is getting less and less in quantity, and more expensive, the space for industrial growth will become smaller and smaller. Since we are committed to developing big industries and leading big industries, it is necessary to calculate the essential elements for the development of these industries, and how these elements are distributed across the world. We need to calculate the output value for each square metre of land, and how many people are needed to produce that value, and take into account housing and living facilities for these people. If these are too expensive for enterprises to afford, the cost is too high, and industry will not develop there.

GOING GLOBAL FOR CHINESE ENTERPRISES: "TO UNDERSTAND LAWS. MONEY IS NOT THE ONLY FACTOR THAT DETERMINES THE INVESTMENT."

Reporter: Do you have any suggestions for Chinese enterprises to go global?

Ren Zhengfei: Firstly, China needs to improve the legal system, where enterprises need to abide by the laws. If you don't act according to the laws in your own country, going global will be hashing and battering. I don't support Chinese enterprises going global blindly. The legal institutions' influence on society is not immediate. It takes decades or even a century to take effect. Secondly, China needs to learn to manage the market economy. Those who survive in the business battles in China are strong enough to compete worldwide. China needs to improve legal and accounting systems, etc. and enable enterprises to go global as strong competitors. Otherwise, enterprises may face a lot of risks and lose everything. I think for Chinese enterprises, the priority is to abide by the legal system and understand the laws. Money is not the only factor that determines the investment.

MAY 9TH, 2016,
XINHUA NEWS AGENCY,
SHENZHEN

Reporter: Zhao Donghui, Li Bin, Liu Shiping, Cai Guozhao, Peng Yong, He Yuxin.